REFLECTIVE HISTORY SERIES

Barbara Finkelstein and William J. Reese, Series Editors

Changing Course

AMERICAN CURRICULUM REFORM IN THE 20th CENTURY

Herbert M. Kliebard

TEACHERS
COLLEGE
PRESS

Teachers College, Columbia University
New York and London

Published by Teachers College Press, 1234 Amsterdam Avenue, New York, NY 10027

These essays are reprinted with editorial modifications by permission. Chapter 1, "Constructing the Concept of Curriculum on the Wisconsin Frontier: How School Restructuring Sustained a Pedagogical Revolution," from *History of Education* 25 (June 1996), and Chapter 7, "Cultural Literacy, or The Curate's Egg," from *Journal of Curriculum Studies* 21 (January–February 1989), by permission of Taylor & Francis Ltd., PO Box 25, Abingdon, Oxfordshire, OX14 3UE, England. Chapter 2, "'That Evil Genius of the Negro Race': Thomas Jesse Jones and Educational Reform," and Chapter 4, "A Century of Growing Antagonism in High School–College Relations," from *Journal of Curriculum and Supervision* 10 (Fall 1994) and 3 (Fall 1987), respectively. Reprinted with permission from the Association for Supervision and Curriculum Development. All rights reserved. Chapter 3, "The *Cardinal Principles* Report as Archaeological Deposit," from *Curriculum Studies* 3 (October 1995). Chapter 5, "Harold Rugg and the Reconstruction of the Social Studies Curriculum: The Treatment of the 'Great War' in His Textbook Series," by Herbert M. Kliebard and Greg Wegner, from *The Formation of School Subjects: The Struggle for Creating an American Institution,* ed. Thomas Popkewitz (New York: Falmer Press, 1987). Chapter 6, "Fads, Fashions, and Rituals: The Instability of Curriculum Change," from *Critical Issues in Curriculum*, ed. Laurel Tanner, Part I, *87th Yearbook of the National Society for the Study of Education* (1988). Chapter 8, "One Kind of Excellence: Ensuring Academic Achievement at La Salle High School," by Herbert M. Kliebard and Calvin R. Stone, from *High School Journal* 76 (October–November 1992). Chapter 9, "Success and Failure in Educational Reform: Are There Historical 'Lessons'?" from *Peabody Journal of Education* 55 (Winter 1988).

Cover photos: Top, traditional classroom, c. 1932, from the collection of the author. Bottom, fourth grade store, University School, The Ohio State University, 1948, courtesy of The Ohio State University Archives.

Library of Congress Cataloging-in-Publication Data

Kliebard, Herbert M.
    Changing course : American curriculum reform in the 20th century / Herbert M. Kliebard.
       p. cm.— (Reflective history series)
    Includes bibliographical references (p.) and index.
    ISBN 0-8077-4221-X (alk. paper) — ISBN 0-8077-4222-8 (alk. paper)
      1. Curriculum planning—United States—History—20th century. 2. Curriculum change—United States—History—20th century. I. Title. II. Series.

LB2806.15 .K59 2002
375'.001'0973—dc21   2001060385

ISBN 0-8077-4221-X (paper)
ISBN 0-8077-4222-8 (cloth)

Printed on acid-free paper
Manufactured in the United States of America

09 08 07 06 05 04 03 02   8 7 6 5 4 3 2 1

Dedicated to Arno A. Bellack
A great mentor and dear friend

Contents

Acknowledgments

This volume is dedicated to Arno A. Bellack, who served as my graduate advisor at Teachers College, Columbia University. When I first met him, I was a young man lacking direction and uncertain of my future. Arno was instrumental in opening up new scholarly and professional vistas for me, especially in the way he encouraged my fledgling efforts in the area of curriculum history. Arno has a rare and wonderful quality—an incredible ability to bring out the best in others. He has continued to perform that function for me over the course of many years. What more can you ask of a mentor and friend?

There are, of course, many others to whom I am indebted. My late wife, Bernice, has always been a mainspring of love and support, and I am afraid I shall never really recover from her loss. My children, Diane and Ken, have always been sources of delight and love as are my grandchildren now.

I also should like to acknowledge the invaluable advice provided by my esteemed colleague William Reese, a series editor for Teachers College Press, who was always available with sound suggestions and criticism as I proceeded on this project. Barry Franklin also has provided invaluable advice over a period of many years. Along those lines, I am deeply indebted to many other colleagues and staff at the University of Wisconsin–Madison. Although I cannot enumerate them all, they are a extraordinary group who have made my professional life especially rewarding in untold ways. The students I have had over the years also deserve special mention. I have been continually inspired by their intellectual curiosity and their fresh outlook on the world of scholarship. Thank you all.

INTRODUCTION

Reform and Change in the American Curriculum

Pessimism about school reform is nothing new. As early as 1922, W. W. Charters, one of the twentieth century's leading curriculum reformers, was already declaring that "the history of American education is a chronicle of fads."[1] Since that time, the failure of educational reform has continued to be the subject of persistent concern and frustration. There is good reason for this. Although curriculum reformers were unusually active over the course of the twentieth century, their actual successes were sporadic and notoriously short-lived. The term *pendulum swing* has become the most widely used characterization of this phenomenon, implying, of course, that educational reform is nothing but a series of backward and forward movements with, in the end, everything remaining in place. Whatever the merits of *pendulum swing* as the controlling metaphor for the course of educational reform, it reflects a profound disillusionment with the enterprise.

In recent years, educational reform, although still very much with us, has taken a decidedly different turn from the efforts that prevailed during most of the twentieth century. Policy makers continue to try to improve school practice, of course, but the most widely touted reform takes the form of specifying rigorous achievement standards accompanied by high-stakes testing.[2] When students do not measure up, school officials are urged to deny them promotion or graduation. Presumably, positive results will ensue if children and youth are so coerced, but the actual outcome of such a policy is not clear. A recent front-page article in the *New York Times* reports that in Arizona, where high stakes testing has been adopted with enthusiasm, 70% of sophomores in a middle-class suburban high school failed the mathematics examination. Statewide, the failure rate was 84%. Needless to say, policy makers are taking such results under advisement. Moreover, Arizona's experience was not an isolated one. California, Maryland, Massachusetts, Delaware, Ohio, Wisconsin, and Alaska also are reconsidering their testing policies,[3] but the impulse to provide what is euphemistically called accountability is politically difficult to resist. The problem is that, in and of itself, testing is not a reform at all; it is at best a measure of success and in the right circumstances may become a spur to reform.

At the same time as this surrogate for educational reform seems to be taking hold, the kinds of pedagogical reform that were prevalent during most of the twentieth century are becoming the subject of not only political but scholarly criticism.

Generally speaking, this re-examination of earlier school reform pursues two rather different paths. One takes the form of a substantial rejection of the pedagogical reforms that were pursued during the so-called progressive era in education on the grounds that they were simply ill-advised to begin with or have had undesirable consequences. Two recent historical works, for example, impart a rather caustic view of the course that school reform has taken in the twentieth century. Even the titles of David Angus and Jeffrey Mirel's *The Failed Promise of the American High School, 1890–1995*[4] and Diane Ravitch's *Left Back: A Century of Failed School Reforms*[5] convey the sense that the concerted efforts to change school practice over a period of many years somehow have gone awry. According to such accounts, it is not simply that many of these reforms failed to accomplish their purposes, but that they were ill-conceived to begin with. To the extent that they have affected school practice, they need to be undone. The second kind of critical examination, best exemplified by David Tyack and Larry Cuban's *Tinkering Toward Utopia: A Century of Public School Reform*,[6] takes a balanced view of the reforms themselves, but undertakes to examine the particular question of why so many well-meaning and even well-conceived reforms failed to make their way into school practice. This line of historical research tends to be less judgmental about the reforms themselves and more concerned with the reasons why some reforms succeeded while others failed to make much of an impact on school practice.

In one sense, the nine essays that constitute this volume reflect both these streams of historical criticism. Some of the essays unquestionably take a dim view of certain of the reforms that were undertaken and focus on their ideological and conceptual shortcomings. Other essays address the reasons why certain reforms collapsed while different ones succeeded, in much the same way that Tyack and Cuban do. In another sense, however, taken as a whole, these essays do not so much render a general verdict on the record of school reform over the past century or so as attempt to differentiate among various kinds of reforms and address the sources of their failure to make a lasting impact. As I hope the essays in this volume convey, reform is not one thing. *Reform* is one of those portmanteau words that incorporates a wide range of efforts, some noble and worthy and some misguided and even reprehensible. Although the word *reform* carries with it nearly universal positive connotations, it should be cause for celebration when certain reforms fail; on the other hand, the failure of some efforts to successfully redress the obvious shortcomings and injustices of schooling is deplorable and in some cases even tragic.

Guiding my efforts to assess the nature of these reforms is a particular view of what has come to be called *progressive education*. As I see it, a good part of the problem of interpreting the nature of curriculum reform over the course of the twentieth century lies in the inclination to lump together disparate and even contradictory reforms under that one familiar label. That tendency invites a global judgment as to the wisdom or folly, success or failure, of a single entity. In other words, it is presumably that entity that needs to be examined and appraised. Rejecting *progressive education* as anything like a unitary enterprise permits a more nuanced view of what actually was going on over that period of time. Some lines of reform during what familiarly is called the progressive era were surely ill-considered to begin with and detrimental in their effect on the education of schoolchildren, while others were not only perspicacious in the way they addressed the persistent problems of schooling but reflected a truly democratic spirit, a force for liberating intelligence, and a strong sense of social justice. It is no cause for celebration when those reforms fail.

There is no question that in the latter part of the nineteenth century and in the first 6 decades or so of the twentieth, reform in the sense of departing from the status quo was in the air. In terms of the curriculum, the status quo was represented by the standard academic subjects such as history, geography, English, mathematics, science, and foreign languages. In terms of teaching, the status quo overwhelmingly took the form of the recitation method (largely textbook based) in which the teacher asked questions and pupils were called upon to respond. With few exceptions, firsthand accounts gathered by the crusading journalist Joseph Mayer Rice point to a pattern of school practice in the late nineteenth and early twentieth centuries that was largely dominated by rote recitation of seemingly trivial factual information drawn, at least loosely, from the academic subjects.[7] There was, in other words, good reason to undertake to change what was by and large a sterile and mindless pattern of schooling.

Some of the efforts to reform this practice took a rather moderate turn. Charles W. Eliot, revered president of Harvard University, for example, sought to give high status to the study of modern foreign languages in secondary schools as opposed to Latin and Greek, on the grounds that modern languages would elicit more interest on the part of students and thereby have a more beneficial effect on their mental functioning.[8] He was also a strong supporter of a wide array of elective subjects in an effort to evoke interest on the part of students. Similarly, over the course of his long career, William Torrey Harris, highly respected superintendent of schools in St. Louis and later long-term U.S. Commissioner of Education, argued for the virtues of teaching academic subjects as a way of initiating children and youth into the great resources of civilization rather than treating school subjects as an array of disjointed facts and skills. What he called the five windows of the soul—arithmetic, geography, history, grammar, and literature—were in his mind ways of opening up the accumulated wisdom of the human race to a new generation.[9]

For other reformers of roughly the same period, these proposals were just too tame. One prominent reformer, William Heard Kilpatrick, for example, sought to substitute the project for the subject as the basic unit in the curriculum.[10] Such a revolutionary change, Kilpatrick believed, could lead to overcoming the passivity of the learner, still a significant problem today, with intelligent action replacing the process of simply storing information. He and his devoted followers initiated a movement that achieved limited success in its time but is barely alive today. By contrast, the movement that became known as social reconstructionism, led by such reformers as George S. Counts and Harold O. Rugg, sought to focus the curriculum on persistent and pressing social problems in an effort to make schools more responsive to social needs and consistent with their conceptions of social justice. Here again, the movement was able to make some modest inroads into schools, but, although something of the spirit of that movement survives in the proposals of a handful of contemporary reformers, its successes in terms of actually affecting school practice were few and far between.

By far the greatest successes were achieved by reformers such as Franklin Bobbitt, W. W. Charters, and David Snedden, who sought to create a supremely functional curriculum guided by the criterion of efficiency. Principles of efficiency were introduced not only to affect day-to-day school practice but to make the curriculum as a whole socially efficient by ensuring that whatever children and youth studied would relate directly to their ability to function in their future adult roles. Subjects that could not be shown to be directly functional in this sense were curtailed, reconstructed, or eliminated, thus reducing waste. A key component of social efficiency ideology was vocationalism, which singled out projected work roles in particular as the principal guideposts for driving the curriculum.[11] Although the aspirations of the social efficiency reformers were not fully realized (they never are), the American curriculum moved substantially in that direction.

With such contrasting visions of how the curriculum should be reformed, it obviously would be futile to try to arrive at global judgments as to reforms generally or to an entity called *progressive education* in particular, either with respect to its feasibility or to its moral and intellectual legitimacy. Rather, one needs to examine the main lines of reform in terms of their guiding theoretical presuppositions as well as their prospective or actual impact on the practical world of schools. When reforms are propelled by such widely disparate social and pedagogical visions as were evident in the so-called progressive era, it becomes virtually impossible to treat them all as if they were of one piece and still do them justice. Sweeping praise or condemnation simply covers up too much. Accordingly, the essays included here, insofar as possible, try to address those distinctive visions in particular terms.

Another theme running through some of the essays is the question of the way in which reforms actually make their way into school practice. Two of the essays, for example, the case study of the one-room Otsego, Wisconsin, school in the nineteenth century and the Rugg series of social studies textbooks in the 1930s, treat the subject in terms of the considerable success that was achieved in those cases, rather than along the more familiar theme of the failure of reform efforts.

My own understanding of what contributes to success and failure in this regard is actually quite similar to the position taken by Tyack and Cuban. Reforms that are inconsistent with the basic structures of schooling (what Tyack and Cuban call "the grammar of schooling"), such as replacing the subject with something else or sharply redefining the roles of teacher and student, tend to collapse even when they meet initial success in terms of implementation. Another way of putting it is that pedagogical reforms either need to be consistent with existing structures or reformers need to undertake ways of altering those structures in order to make them compatible with the pedagogical reforms. Otherwise, the reforms, whatever their merits on other grounds, simply will be disgorged. Incidentally, the reverse also is probably true. The introduction of an important structural change such as age stratification—as in the one-room Otsego school in the first essay—can have a profound effect on the pedagogical process. Similarly, it seems perfectly reasonable to assume that the introduction of a structural change such as high-stakes testing would affect in very important ways both what is taught and the manner in which teaching goes forward.

Another theme that runs through some of the essays is the connection between educational reform and the social context in which it is proposed and implemented. It almost goes without saying that the fate of reform is affected by the social and political climate of the period. Reform movements, such as those just enumerated, find strength or weakness depending on their compatibility with the tenor of the times. It is probably fair to say that none of these movements becomes totally extinguished; rather, they gain momentum and favor when the times are right and then lose their impetus and fall into disrepute when the social and political context changes. The ideas that prompted social reconstructionism, for example, existed before the period of the Great Depression but attracted relatively little attention. Once massive social dislocation set in and severe economic problems came to the fore in the 1930s, the idea that curriculum reform somehow could become a vehicle for addressing those problems gained currency. When social and economic problems eased, at least in the public consciousness, social reconstructionism as a force for school reform lost momentum.

The arrangement of the essays in this volume is roughly chronological in terms of the periods under consideration. They range from the period just after the Civil War to contemporary times. In terms of subject matter, they include specific reforms such as Thomas Jesse Jones's efforts to reconstruct the social studies in line with prevailing conceptions of social worth and E.D. Hirsch's advocacy of the concept of cultural literacy as a way of addressing the widespread lack of cultural knowledge on the part of many schoolchildren and citizens generally. In some cases, the focus is more general, such as the way in which the *Cardinal Principles* report reflected a broad range of reform efforts with one predominating ideology, social efficiency, and the long-standing insistence that college-entrance requirements have posed a major obstacle to secondary-school reform over the course of many years. The book concludes with an effort to see whether there are any lessons to be learned from the historical record. Each of the essays is preceded by its own brief introduction, which attempts to relate the particular concerns expressed in the essay to broad themes of reform and change in American schooling.

CHAPTER 1

Constructing the Concept of Curriculum on the Wisconsin Frontier: How School Restructuring Sustained a Pedagogical Revolution

The failure of educational reform is such a widespread phenomenon that it is easy to overlook significant change when it occurs and even when a pedagogical revolution takes place. Once instituted, practices associated with such successful change often may, over time, appear so normal and natural that even a significant break with past practice escapes notice. This case study of a Wisconsin one-room school traces the course of a major redirection in school practice that affected both the process of teaching and the emergence of what we now mean by a curriculum. One of the fundamental changes in this Otsego, Wisconsin, rural school is the dramatic shift in the teacher's role from "keeping school," that is, from overseeing or monitoring pupil behavior, to teaching in the sense of actually providing instruction. The related major shift entails a movement away from the textbook as controlling the subject matter of study to a curriculum entailing a planned sequence of learning activities replete with objectives.

What were the particular circumstances and conditions that led to such a major upheaval in school practice? One clue lies in the quotation from a 1901 address by John Dewey which opens the essay. Dewey points to the crucial but commonly underestimated significance of the relationship between organizational structure and pedagogical change. Following this lead, the essay then becomes an effort to map out the structural changes in Wisconsin's rural schools during this period, changes that led to the sustenance and even the initiation of far-reaching and lasting pedagogical reforms. These changes entail such seemingly mundane organizational features as the length of the school year and the manner in which teachers were hired, but, as I hope this essay demonstrates, these structural features had much to do with undergirding what amounted to a pedagogical revolution.

By 1901, John Dewey was already troubled about the failure of many educational reforms. With astonishing regularity, promising pedagogical innovations had made their appearance, enjoyed a brief day in the sun, and then quietly vanished. In attempting to account for this phenomenon, Dewey called attention to what he believed to be at least one source of this failure—an incompatibility between the organization and management of schools and many pedagogical reforms:

It is easy to fall into the habit of regarding the mechanics of school organization and administration as something comparatively external and indifferent to educational purposes and ideals. We think of the grouping of children in classes, the arrangement of grades, the machinery by which the course of study is made out and laid down, the method by which it is carried into effect, the system of selecting teachers and of assigning them to their work, of paying and promoting them, as, in a way, matters of mere practical convenience and expediency. We forget that it is precisely such things as these that really control the whole system, even on its distinctively educational side. No matter what is the accepted precept and theory, no matter what the legislation of the school board or the mandate of the school superintendent, the reality of education is found in the personal and face-to-face contact of teacher and child. The conditions that underlie and regulate this contact dominate the educational situation.[1]

This pivotal connection between school organization and management on one hand and what Dewey called "the face-to-face contact of teacher and child" on the other is underappreciated even today. On the surface at least, such matters as the structure of the school year and the organization of pupils into groups of like achievement and expectations seem to be matters "of mere practical convenience and expediency," but these structural features of schooling, it appears, are in fact intimately bound to the very core of the educational process.[2] If Dewey's hypothesis is correct, then pedagogical changes, even dramatic ones, may be sustained or undermined depending on whether the organization and management of schools are compatible with those changes.

What follows is an attempt to trace the relationship between organizational restructuring and the emergence of two revolutionary pedagogical changes, derived largely from data relating to a single country school in Columbia County, Wisconsin, in the latter half of the nineteenth century. The evidence suggests that these closely interrelated pedagogical changes, (1) the appearance of a concept of curriculum that was above and beyond what was dictated by the textbook and (2) what is called here *ensemble teaching* (as distinct from teaching as monitoring individual recitations), are intimately connected with a major reconstruction of the management and organization of schooling across the State of Wisconsin and in the United States generally. That organizational change, age stratification, it would appear, prompted fundamental alterations both in how the curriculum was conceptualized and in how teachers taught. Although it was surely not the first instance either of age stratification or of the emergence of a modern conception of curriculum, nor was it the first time that teachers reached beyond the common practice of hearing individual recitations as the predominant form of teaching, it is one early and vivid illustration of how structural changes undergirded a major reconstruction of prevailing conceptions of curriculum and teaching.

CURRICULUM AND TEACHING IN COUNTRY SCHOOLS
ON THE MIDDLE BORDER

At its most fundamental level, what we call the curriculum embodies what is to be taught, and what we call teaching refers to those actions that a teacher undertakes in order to implement the curriculum. When seen in such broad terms, there was certainly such a thing as a curriculum in country schools of the period just after the Civil War in the American Midwest, and there were obviously actions undertaken by the teacher that could reasonably be called teaching; but the forms they assumed were considerably different in character from our modern and more elaborated understanding of those concepts.

In the case of curriculum, there were, of course, subjects, and it is subjects that were (and remain today) the basic building blocks from which a curriculum is constructed. What was called a subject then, however, was so intimately tied to the textbook used to convey that subject that the line between subject and textbook was virtually indistinguishable. This correspondence between subject and text goes back at least to the colonial period in America. In fact, during the seventeenth and eighteenth centuries, the names of the subjects and the names of the textbooks were often one and the same. The subject of reading could be represented as the New England Primer, the subject of arithmetic as James Hodder's "Hodder's arithmetick, or that necessary art made most easy," and the subject of Latin as Cheever's Accidence or the Colloquies of Corderius. When a school undertook to publish its curriculum, it often was recorded as a list of names of textbooks.[3]

For most of the nineteenth century, the curriculum as the object of professional concern in the United States consisted largely of discussion of the benefits presumably derived from the study of the subjects, including, here and there, some disagreement as to the respective value of the subjects to be taught. To a large extent, the actual content of these subjects as subjects was ill-defined. When the *Wisconsin Journal of Education* was launched in 1856, for example, the inaugural issue included the first of a series of four articles devoted to the course of study. The author, identified as J. L. P. (actually J. L. Pickard of Platteville, Wisconsin), waxed poetic over certain subjects of study. Reading was described as "the mouth of the mind, through which must be received all its nourishment."[4] With respect to the subject of penmanship, Pickard declared, "Words written are but the clothing of ideas"; whereas in the case of arithmetic, "No other study has so wide a range of influence or exerts such a power in the formation of character."[5] Beyond the idea that these subjects had such salubrious properties, there was little to guide the teacher in actually teaching the subjects. By implication at least, what the teacher actually taught in their name was set forth in the textbook.

If the curriculum was defined by the textbooks that children brought with them to school, then teaching in country schools consisted largely of hearing children recite from those textbooks. What is more, the lack of uniformity in textbooks, even within a single school, made the process of teaching difficult to manage. Not only were textbooks not supplied by country schools in the early part of the nineteenth century, but they were different from one child to the next. Even children of the same age and school experience would recite individually on various subjects from the textbooks that they happened to bring with them to school.[6] As Barbara Finkelstein observes, "In the one-room schools of the countryside . . . where students of varying ages, backgrounds and levels achievement brought their own texts to class, the teachers treated each pupil as unique—making individual assignments, hearing individual recitations, and rendering individual appraisals."[7] She cites, for example, the recollections of an Indiana farmer who recalls his country schooling in the 1840s:

> There was no program to be followed, no order of exercises, no system. When a scholar felt that he had studied his lesson well and was prepared to recite, he would take his book in hand, and go forward to the master's desk. (James Baldwin, quoted *ibid*.)

In short, there was no course of study in the contemporary sense. Teaching as well was considerably different from modern practice. By and large, when country teachers taught, it took the form of making assignments from a textbook for each student and then listening to the student recite that lesson as time permitted. To be sure, a teacher might engage his or her class in a group activity every now and then, such as group singing or a spelling bee, but teaching was largely a process of monitoring individual recitations from a bewildering array of different textbooks.

While the ingenious or daring teacher could depart from this pattern, for the most part, learning a lesson meant committing some portion of a textbook to memory. As Mary Bradford recalled of her schooling in the 1860s, "To recite meant to repeat the words of a book; to study meant to commit to memory words for such a recitation. The one who possessed the best word-memory was the most satisfactory pupil."[8] Although group recitation undoubtedly played some role, a typical day of teaching consisted of children marching one-by-one to the teacher's desk to recite their lessons. Keeping order rather than teaching was seen as the teacher's main duty. In one joint district school in Columbia County, Wisconsin, for example, where visitors to the school in the 1870s were asked to record their reactions, the comments centered almost exclusively on issues of order and management rather than teaching. Over the course of about a decade, the only visitor's comment related to teaching per se as opposed to discipline or order was "Recitations good."[9]

For a time, this practice of teaching as hearing individual recitations seemed immutable. To a large extent, that pattern of teaching was perpetuated by the fact that the teachers themselves had been taught through textbook recitation, and, lacking formal training for the most part, they taught in the only way they knew how. The practice of recitation also was reinforced by the reigning pedagogical theory of the day, mental discipline. Since the object of education according to that theory was to strengthen certain innate faculties of the mind, what could be more efficacious in that regard than to set up rigorous muscle-building exercises for the children to recite? Fundamental changes in curriculum and teaching awaited a constituent alteration in the management and organization of schooling.

SUMMER AND WINTER TERMS AT THE OTSEGO VILLAGE SCHOOL, 1867–1880

Many of our management and organizational practices with regard to schooling are now so well established that it is difficult not to take them for granted. Take, for example, the modern practice of organizing instruction within the context of a school year. The school year not only serves as the calendar unit during which school services are available; it also represents the unit of time for which teacher contracts are offered. It is the organizational framework for what Dewey called "the system of selecting teachers and assigning them to their work." In the period just after the Civil War on the Wisconsin frontier, however, the school year was anything but an established fact. Rather, country schools were organized around two distinct and separate periods of schooling, the winter term and the summer term. When interested citizens in School District No. 3 of Otsego, Wisconsin, for example, gathered for their annual meeting, one of the main items of business was to set the beginning and ending dates of each of the two terms. Accordingly, on September 2, 1867, those citizens of Otsego School District No. 3 in attendance voted to raise $285 in taxes for the ensuing year, $160 to cover teacher wages and $125 for the contingent fund. They then set the starting dates of the two terms as November 1 and April 1, with each term running for 4 months.[10] In ensuing years, however, the summer term was often shorter than the winter term, sometimes only 2½ months in duration.

Until 1880, each term and hence each teacher contract was subject to the time spans set at each annual meeting. In Otsego's one-room school, the summer term usually was set to begin after the spring planting of the potato crop, and the winter term would begin after harvest. Generally, as David Angus, Jeffrey Mirel, and Maris Vinovskis put it, "Going to school in the country was a seasonal activity contingent on the need for agricultural labor at home."[11] In fact, the older farm boys often would attend school only in the winter term. Since these boys were reputed to be obstreperous, winter terms were regarded as more difficult to teach, and, from time to time, Otsego residents as well as citizens guiding country schools elsewhere voted specifically to hire a male teacher for the winter term and a fe-

male teacher for the summer term. In School District No. 5 in the nearby town of
Scott, for example, specifying male teachers for the winter term and female teachers
for the summer term was the rule rather than the exception.[12]

Table 1.1 indicates the variation in the beginning dates of the school term in
the Otsego school over a 14-year span. Derived from actual school contracts and
minutes of meetings, the data also convey the considerable variation in salaries of
teachers and in teacher hiring practices, especially with respect to the discontinu-
ity from one term to the next.[13]

What is especially striking about this picture compared with modern school
organization is the discreteness of each term. Although city schools began awarding
school-year contracts earlier, the concept of a school year as we know it today
seems not to have existed in Otsego prior to 1880. Otsego was unexceptional in
this regard. In rural schools generally, teacher contracts typically were drawn up
individually for each of two terms of 3 to 4 months. Although this appears to be
a rather trivial detail relating to the vagaries of school management rather than to
pedagogical demands, it is tied in rather profound ways to how children were
taught. Because different teachers usually were hired for each of the terms, children would experience almost no coherence with respect to their studies from one
term to the next. One small-town newspaper editor recalling his school experiences in the 1860s in Berks County, Pennsylvania, for example, reported that in
his seven terms of public schooling he had had seven teachers.[14] In such circumstances, since there was no curriculum to guide the teacher, what little continuity
there was came from the textbooks that the pupils brought with them to school.

Of the 25 different teachers serving in the one-room Otsego Village School
between 1867 and 1880, only Susan Waters, Jennie Mitchell, Celia Pulver, and
J. B. Meridth served as many as two terms, and, even then, each of their contracts
was awarded for just one term at a time. Susan Waters, Jennie Mitchell, and Celia
Pulver were the only teachers to serve two consecutive terms. Over the 13-year
period prior to 1880, no teacher was hired for as many as three terms. In general,
then, children in Otsego School District No. 3 were almost certain to confront a
new teacher with each new term. This changed abruptly on August 30, 1880. At
their annual meeting, the assembled citizens took the unprecedented step of passing a motion "that the board hire a female teacher for the whole year." It was not,
then, until Hannah Slattery obtained a contract covering both terms at once that
the situation changed and the modern concept of a school year began to emerge
in Otsego School District No. 3. In the following year, for example, a similar motion was passed to hire a teacher for the full year, this time specifically authoriz-
ing the board to hire either a male or a female teacher.[15]

This departure from a long-standing practice may have been signaled a year
earlier when the opening date for the winter term in 1879 was set at September 8.
As the table indicates, this was approximately 4 to 7 weeks earlier than the customary starting date at Otsego. Following the new pattern, Hannah Slattery's first

Table 1.1. Starting Dates and Salaries of Otsego Schoolteachers

Term	Beginning Date	Teacher's Name [a]	Salary (dollars)
Winter 1867	Nov. 5	Susan Waters	40 per month
Summer 1868	—	Susan Waters	40 per month
Winter 1868	Nov. 9	Jennie Mitchell	35 per month
Summer 1869	Apr. 27	Jennie Mitchell	40 per month
Winter 1869	Nov. 15	Cyrus R. Heuton*	40 per month
Summer 1870	—	—	—
Winter 1870	—	—	—
Summer 1871	May 1	Jennie Grout	27 per month
Winter 1871	Nov. 13	A. W. Grout*	40 per month
Summer 1872	Apr. 29	Nora Waters	30 per month
Winter 1872	Nov. 18	John Grout	45 per month
Summer 1873	May 5	Viola Nicholson	25 per month
Winter 1873	Nov. 17	Daniel W. Hall*	40 per month
Summer 1874	Apr. 27	Cora A. Downs*	25 per month
Winter 1874	Nov. 23	John E. Grant	200 for 17 weeks
Summer 1875	May 3	Celia S. Pulver*	17 for 16 weeks
Winter 1875	Nov. 15	Celia S. Pulver*	120 for 17 weeks
Summer 1876	May 1	Evelyn Todd	20 per month
Winter 1876	Nov. 13	Frances Palmer*	25 per month
Summer 1877	Apr. 30	Mary A. James*	18 per month
Winter 1877	Nov. 20	William E. Ritter	30 per month
Summer 1878	Apr. 22	N. G. Dunning*	18 per month
Winter 1878	Nov. 18	J. B. Meridth*	38 per month
Summer 1879	Apr. 13	Celia P. Randalls*	18 per month
Winter 1879	Sept. 8	Nellie Gabrielson [b]	20 per month
Winter 1879	Dec. 1	J. B. Meridth [c]	33 per month
Winter 1879	Dec. 28	Charles Williams [d]	30 per month
Summer 1880	Apr. 19	Carrie Amis	20 per month
Winter 1880	Sept. 6	Hannah Slattery*	20 per month

Note. From Herbert M. Kliebard, "The Feminization of Teaching on the American Frontier: Keeping School in Otsego, Wisconsin, 1867–1880," *Journal of Curriculum Studies* 27 (September–October 1995).

[a] Asterisks indicate Otsego residents.

[b] Nellie Gabrielson's contract was for only the first 2 months of the 1879 winter term.

[c] J. B. Meridth's contract called for his services only in the month of December.

[d] Charles Williams taught the remaining 2 ½ months of the 1879 winter term.

[handwritten] ✱females were paid less than men no matter winter or summer?

pils into groups called grades and the development of a defined program of studies for each of those groups, therefore, were intimately connected. When Pickett undertook to spell out his scheme of classification, for example, he did so by setting forth what we now think of as curricular objectives for each of the grades. Part of the problem he sought to address was the inexperience of country teachers. To a considerable extent, they were deemed incapable of devising a course of study. As Pickett put it, "For a long time to come most of our country schools must be taught by those who are comparatively young and inexperienced, and consequently in this cause of so great moment [creation of a course of instruction] and embracing so much difficulty and complication, we cannot expect success without system, nor without making that system so plain that a teacher though a mere youth cannot err therein."[17] In short, he was recommending that teachers be given a curriculum to follow as a corrective for the youth, inexperience, or lack of resourcefulness on their part.

Thus, in first-grade arithmetic, Pickett stipulated among other objectives, "To count the number forward or backward," and "To add one to, or subtract it from any number, from one to fifty,"[18] and, in geography, "the class should . . . learn the meaning of a linear inch, a square inch, a linear foot, linear rod, square rod, of the acre, quarter section, section and town." These learning expectations amounted to a curriculum independent of a textbook. Of equal importance was the fact that these objectives were obviously meant to apply to categories of students—grade levels—not to individuals. Pickett specified, for example, that in teaching geography, the teacher should draw on the blackboard a map of the town, indicating such features as principal streams and bodies of water, valleys, swamps, schoolhouses, churches, and roads.[19] Clearly, A. P.'s conception of curriculum was dramatically different from that of his colleague, J. L. P., as expressed only a few years before. Subjects were no longer just generalized purveyors of desirable qualities of mind or character; they were the repositories of specific things that had to be learned in a kind of regular progression.

In 1879, demands for grading in Wisconsin culminated in State Superintendent William C. Whitford's widely distributed plan for grading (classifying) the pupils in Wisconsin schools. As was the case with earlier proposals, grading, as interpreted by Whitford, presupposed not just periodic examinations but a *course of study,* that is, a suitable set of learning activities associated with a particular grade level. Specific standards of achievement in the common branches of study were to be tied to each of three proposed levels: the primary form, the middle form, and the upper form.[20] In presenting his justification for the new plan, Whitford specified, as one advantage, that a "definite end can be presented for the pupils to attain in pursuing their studies, and a fixed course of action covering several years to which they must conform in reaching this end." Moreover, movement from one grade to the next would "be accurately determined as the result of an efficient system of examinations."[21] In short, grading (classification of students) implied anticipated levels of achievement for each grade or form; anticipated levels of achievement implied examinations to determine the appropriate grade and appropriate progress; and, all together, this implied a curriculum above and beyond what amounted to a place marker in a textbook. The concept of grading, in other words, required a new way of thinking about the curriculum.

It could hardly be a coincidence that new state regulations requiring grading of pupils were first promulgated only a year before Otsego School District No. 3 undertook to award Hannah Slattery its first full school-year contract. Whether teachers are hired for just one term or for a whole school year seems to be of less than earth-shaking significance, but grading of pupils as a managerial change carried with it the seeds of how the very process of education was conceived of. It provided both the structural framework and the impetus by which continuity in the curriculum could be maintained from one term to the next. The awarding of Hannah Slattery's contract for the 1880–81 school year was a signal not only that major organizational changes were being instituted but that significant pedagogical changes were afoot on the Wisconsin frontier and in the United States generally. Whether the organizational changes actually provided the impetus for the pedagogical change or vice versa is difficult to establish. It is clear, nevertheless, that the pedagogical and organizational changes are critically interdependent.

Once learning expectations were set by grade level rather than by individual textbook, the very activity of teaching had to change. With pupils organized into groups of like expectations, the teacher was obligated to teach them as a group rather than hearing individuals recite. In fact, the trend in the direction of group instruction was marked by the growing trend in country schools toward using uniform textbooks for each grade. In Otsego School District No. 3, for example, the first recorded instance of textbooks formally adopted by the board of education occurred on November 18, 1878.[22] It seems likely, then, that the three almost simultaneous organizational changes—Otsego's first uniform textbook adoption in 1878, Superintendent Whitford's edict requiring grading in Wisconsin's schools in 1879, and Otsego's decision to award the first two-term teacher contract in 1880—are related phenomena. They are all consistent with the trend toward greater continuity in the curriculum and therefore toward uniformity in instruction.

Significantly, the practice of grading even in one-room schools was not by any means restricted to country schools in Wisconsin. In an address delivered before the Kansas State Teachers' Association in 1878, Henry Clay Speer, then superintendent of schools in Atchison, Kansas, and later state superintendent, made a similar call for a clear classification of pupils in country schools. Speer was unambiguous as to the implications of grading for the curriculum. "What is arithmetic?" he asked; his answer was that "it is time these questions were defined somewhere else than in text books." The "somewhere else" clearly was the centralized state bureaucracy. Moreover, Speer obviously was referring not simply to designating the subjects to be studied; he had in mind the actual curriculum, much as the term is used today.

One thing that made Speer's address so striking was his blunt justification for advocating this course of action. He simply had no faith that teachers had either the training or the ingenuity to devise their own courses of study. This had to be done for them by true professionals like himself. "It is utterly senseless," he declared, "to put teachers in the work of artists." Designing the school curriculum, in other words, was the province neither of teachers nor of textbooks but of a handful of professionally trained specialists. Teaching was one thing and devising what to teach was another. Teachers, Speer asserted, are "master workmen . . . not architects. . . . There is no genius wanted. Good intelligent, discreet teachers are needed."[23] Here, then, is an early indication of what was to become a major feature of American schooling in the twentieth century: the virtual isolation of the design of the formal curriculum from its execution in the classroom.

By 1887, grading had already gained national acceptance. In an address before the Department of Superintendence in Washington, D. C., the state superintendent of public instruction in Indiana, J. W. Holcome, treated ungraded country schools as a thing of the past, and with that change, in his view, there emerged such a thing as a systematically organized curriculum. He cited, for example, a communication from a county superintendent stating, "A few years ago, what a boy studied was determined by his own caprice or by family tradition and custom. The teacher, confronted by forty or fifty pupils, found as many different courses of study, and was compelled to pass day after day in giving individual lessons to individual pupils. In such a school much time and energy were wasted, the greatest amount of labor being required to produce the smallest result." To, Holcome, the issue was no longer one of policy but of implementation. In his mind, grading in country schools was similar to grading in city schools, requiring only certain adjustments. Taking his own state as typical of the country, he reported that 82% of the teachers were employed in country schools, and 72% of the children were educated there rather than in cities.[24] With the extension of grading to rural America, it was now clearly becoming the standard practice nationally.

In the discussion that followed the Indiana superintendent's speech, the superintendent of schools in Columbia, South Carolina, concurred. "In most of the States, if not all," he said, "there is already a system of gradation in the schools from the lowest primary into the colleges, constituting a ladder upon the rungs of which the city boy may mount from the gutter of degradation to the pinnacles of usefulness and honor." He deplored the fact that children in country schools in the past had been asked to go over the same lessons in their textbooks for five consecutive years with five different teachers.[25] Superintendent Speer from Kansas, arriving too late to hear the main address in its entirety, reiterated his pessimism regarding the ability of the country teacher to create a course of study under the new grading system. "The average teacher of the country school," he asserted, "is not a man or woman upon whom you can depend for the development of the course of study. That is why I say it belongs to the State superintendent."[26] While it would be an obvious exaggeration to claim that the new class of education professionals actually was created by the system of grading, it is fair to say that an emerging class of professionals, consciously or subconsciously, saw in grading a splendid opportunity to centralize the control of public schooling and thereby to enhance their own status.

By 1898, when the first book on grading was published, the classification of students into grades in both city and country schools had proceeded to such an extent that the author, William J. Shearer, felt obligated to propose ways of achieving a measure of flexibility within the classification structure. Shearer, a former country schoolteacher and at the time superintendent of schools in Elizabeth, New Jersey, attributed the origin of the idea in the United States to John Philbrick, who initiated the first graded school in 1847. By 1860, Shearer claimed, most cities and large towns had already adopted the practice. Writing in the 1890s, and acknowledging that grading was then common in country schools as well, Shearer reported that "thoughtful educators are studying this problem as never before, and are planning to strangle the demon of uniformity."[27] In general, he recommended a shorter class interval (one term) rather than the more common whole-year classification and was highly critical of the tendency in country schools to limit classification to only three forms. Whatever the particular scheme of classification, however, it is clear that the spread of grading first to cities and then to country schools over the course of half a century had been nothing short of spectacular. Obviously, such a phenomenon was closely related to the rise in the student population at both the elementary and secondary levels. In fact, the emergence of mass popular education helps explain why age stratification arose first in cities and only later in rural schools like Otsego's.

TRANSFORMATION OF THE OTSEGO SCHOOL

Whatever may have been the motivation of the new class of education professionals for insisting on age grading in the schools of Wisconsin and for simultaneously creating the concept of a curriculum that went beyond textbook recitation, the effects were revolutionary. Records for the one-room school for Otsego School District No. 3 in the first few years of the twentieth century paint a far different picture of what school was like for the inhabitants of country schools from what it was before 1880.

The most obvious difference was the greater continuity in studies from one term to the next. This was made possible by the fact that, to a much larger extent than earlier, the same teacher taught both semesters. Unfortunately, the records of Otsego School District No. 3 are not as complete after 1880 as in the years before, but they do indicate that Hannah Slattery was still drawing her teacher's wages as late as 1882. A 3-year tenure for a teacher at the Otsego school was absolutely unheard of only a few years earlier. In general, the period from 1880 to 1905 seems to have been a transitional one at Otsego, with teachers sometimes staying on for as many as 3 years, followed by a reversion to individual-term hiring.[28] During the mid- to late 1880s and the early 1890s, for example, there appears to have been a temporary reversion to term-to-term hiring of teachers. Christina Crossman, however, began teaching at the school in 1893 and, although a male teacher was hired for the 1894 winter term, she was still recorded as drawing wages as late as 1896. In 1905, Jessie M. Ellis was hired and remained until 1908, and her replacement, Della Curtis, stayed for 2 years. Country school teaching was anything but a long-term career for most teachers until well into the twentieth century, but it was no longer a strictly interim occupation of only a few months duration.

Beyond the length of the teachers' tenure at the Otsego Village School, there was also an evident transformation in the nature of their work. Beginning in 1905 in Otsego, *Harvey's District School Register* was used to record not only student data such as age, grade classification, and attendance but also notations as to what the various classes or forms (primary, middle, and upper) were doing in the various subjects of study. While Jessie Ellis's notations are somewhat sketchy, they do provide some idea as to how the work of teaching had been transformed over the previous quarter-century.

To be sure, the textbook continued to play a large part in instruction, as it does today, and there were frequent references to where groups of children stood with respect to a particular textbook; but there was also clear evidence that Miss Ellis ventured beyond recitation from the textbook, despite the fact that she was obligated to teach 45 students in the three forms during the 1905–06 school year. In the upper form, for example, eight students were recorded as having been given "exercises on foods, healthy habits of cleanliness and the effects of narcotics on the system." There are indications of "work from charts and black board" in arithmetic for seven students, and another group of seven is recorded as having studied "Current events including important Federal officers . . . and the names of these." Moreover, there were "Original practical problems" given, as well as practice in "Commercial forms" to a group of four. Despite the obvious logistical problems in handling so large a class, it is clear that individual recitation had given way to some extent to ensemble teaching that did not always reflect direct instruction from a textbook.

By 1908, Miss Ellis included in her records supplementary reading from library books, map drawing, and letter writing, and there are persistent references to reading words and sentences from the blackboard and cards. Eight students in 1908 planted seeds and made observations as they sprouted. The students participating in each of these activities were recorded by number as they appear in the class roster at the beginning of the register. From the tenor of the notations, it is evident that a major purpose of the records was to ensure that there would be continuity for these groups of students from one year to the next. With group instruction and a curriculum independent of the textbook in place, it was no longer possible to rely on the page number in the textbook as the only indicator of where each pupil stood academically. In short, major pedagogical changes had taken place in the way children were taught at Otsego over the space of a few years, and the direction of these changes is reflective of the now widespread practice of age stratification.

A PEDAGOGICAL REVOLUTION

With so many things happening at the same time, it is difficult to establish a strict chronological rendering of these remarkable changes in country schools, but the logical connections seem clear:

1. An organizational change, grading (age stratification), requires children to be grouped according to like achievement and expectations.
2. Grading cannot really function effectively without a curriculum that expresses common achievement expectations for clusters of students. In this way, the grip of the textbook as curriculum is loosened.
3. In these circumstances, ensemble teaching is supported, with a corresponding decline in teaching as monitoring of individual recitations from textbooks.
4. The new conception of the teacher's role requires another organizational change, longer-term contracts for teachers, so that continuity in the curriculum can be fostered from one term to the next. Teachers also are obligated to keep records of student progress in the event of a change of teachers.

This intimate interrelationship between management and organization on one hand and pedagogical change on the other is exactly what Dewey was talking about in 1901. In fact, as Dewey saw it, it is, if anything, organizational factors (in this case, the new state regulation requiring grading of pupils) that "really control" the pedagogical side. In a sense, then, the Otsego, Wisconsin, case and related data may be seen as offering empirical evidence in support of Dewey's contention.

What happened on the Wisconsin frontier, however, was by no means an isolated phenomenon. Grading and with it a new conception of curriculum was sweeping the United States in the latter part of the nineteenth century. By the time of the National Education Association's Committee of Ten report on secondary school studies in 1893 and the Committee of Fifteen's report on elementary school studies in 1895, the association of a distinct curriculum with various grade levels was simply taken for granted. David Hamilton also has identified the emergence of the concept of "class" with the term *curriculum* in a European context. "Class," Hamilton says, "emerged not as a substitute for school, but, strictly speaking, to identify subdivisions within 'schools.'"[29] What Hamilton calls class and what in Wisconsin was called grading, therefore, amount to the same thing—what Dewey called "the grouping of children in classes." The two terms specify a cluster of pupils within the same school defined according to common expectations as to standards of achievement. Necessarily, there had to be a curriculum that embodied those common expectations.

Grading, in other words, created the structural framework for a curriculum in the modern sense to emerge. At a minimum, grading implied that learning expectations exist, above and beyond textbooks, for groups of students to master at a more or less uniform rate, as A. P. was beginning to articulate in 1863. While a curriculum could still be text-dependent in a particular school, especially one with a uniform textbook policy, a curriculum independent of the textbook was necessary to guide instruction across schools and school districts, since textbooks most likely would be different in different schools in a given state. Since the creation of a curriculum is tied to the notion of school *systems*, it began, naturally enough, in urban school districts and spread only later to country schools. Even in urban centers, then, it seems likely that what we think of today as a curriculum is a phenomenon of the latter part of the nineteenth century and one directly associated with the grouping of students into grades.

Ensemble teaching or what Hamilton refers to as "simultaneous recitation" was an equally revolutionary innovation.[30] By virtue of having several students grouped according to like characteristics as to academic achievement, it became plausible to offer the same instruction to a group of pupils. In ensemble teaching, the teacher could still rely on the textbook, of course, but he or she needed to interact with a cluster of pupils—not simply with individual pupils serially. While the practice of hearing individual recitations unquestionably continued, the nature of teaching gradually began to assume a significant new dimension.

Conceiving of curriculum and teaching in new ways, in turn, required further organizational change. Neither the new concept of curriculum nor that of ensemble teaching makes sense without assuming regular attendance on the part of pupils over a sustained and reasonably uniform period of instruction. The new expectation was that the group stay together. For all intents and purposes, grades were semipermanent units, and their creation by state mandate in 1879 marked the beginning of the end of single-term contracts as the basis of teacher employment. Hannah Slattery's unprecedented academic-year contract in Otsego in 1880 is but one visible manifestation of that organizational change. As long as children on the Wisconsin frontier could return to school after a 6- or 7-month hiatus and simply resume their recitations with the next lesson in the textbook, no concept of school year was necessary; but a pupil grouped with others needed the continuity of a school year and sustained instruction in order to progress with that group. Single-term contracts re-emerged here and there after the introduction of grading in Otsego and elsewhere, but that practice was doomed in the end.

The issue, however, goes well beyond whether teachers were given contracts for only one term or for longer periods. In district schools, the very notion of what it meant to be a teacher began to undergo transformation around 1880 in conjunction with the growing acceptance of changing conceptions of both curriculum and teaching. Longer periods of continuous service for teachers and the idea of a school year rather than a 2-, 3-, or 4-month term as the basic span of instructional time were just outward signs of that larger transformation. With the growing acceptance of the notion that curriculum design was a critical part of the pedagogical process, influential administrators and policy makers began to appropriate that crucial responsibility for themselves. Curriculum making was seen as an activity requiring a technical skill or perhaps a level of intelligence beyond that of the ordinary teacher, as Superintendent Speer and other administrators continually maintained. Thus, teachers were, on one hand, being asked to engage in the more difficult task of ensemble teaching, and, on the other, they were being asked to implement a curriculum dictated not strictly by a textbook but, ironically, by another external authority. This transfer of the important curriculum-making function carried with it significant implications with regard to the status of the largely female teaching force vis-à-vis the predominantly male administrators.[31]

The question then arises as to why the idea of a curriculum beyond the textbook should emerge at this time. No single-factor explanation is entirely persuasive, but one thing is certain: A curriculum is a useful device for creating and maintaining bureaucratic control. The modern idea of a curriculum emerged at a time when popular education in country schools and in cities as well was burgeoning. How long could a system of popular education be managed efficiently when teachers popped helter-skelter in and out of the system, and pupils, more or less, did likewise? Furthermore, the fact that the curriculum was determined primarily by the textbooks that the children happened to bring with them to school stood in the way of centralized management.

In the interest of efficient regulation, educational policy making also had to be rescued from the vagaries of district control then in the hands of what Wayne Fuller calls "educators in overalls" and vested in a central authority represented by an emerging professional class.[32] This could be accomplished in part by transferring the power to certify teachers from hundreds of local town superintendents, to relatively few county superintendents, as was done by the Wisconsin legislature in 1861; but it was also abetted by creating such powerful new concepts as grouping (class) and curriculum. As Hamilton observes in relation to the effect of the introduction of those concepts in Europe, "Teaching and learning became, for good or ill, more open to external scrutiny and control."[33]

Whether or not political control of schooling was indeed the motivating force behind the new grading regulation is actually of less significance than the effect. What is crucially important is that the locus of control in country schools, like urban schools before them, was in fact being shifted from independent citizens and becoming embedded in an emerging bureaucratic framework run, for the most part, by a new breed of professional educators. Once this new bureaucratic structure began to take hold, it generated its own dynamic, and with that development far-reaching pedagogical practices consistent with the new organizational structure were reinforced and extended. It is in this sense that the grouping of pupils in a school into subdivisions called grades, forms, or classes; the appearance of an expanded, more complex concept of curriculum; the practice of ensemble teaching; and the introduction of a school year for pupils as well as the awarding of long-term contracts to teachers were all of one piece.

CHAPTER 2

"That Evil Genius of the Negro Race": Thomas Jesse Jones and Educational Reform

Beginning around the turn of the twentieth century, reform efforts began to reflect a growing professionalization of the curriculum field. The reforms that were being advocated and initiated tended to reflect the ideologies and social outlook of such key actors in that process as Franklin Bobbitt, W. W. Charters, Clarence Kingsley, and David Snedden. Through a critical examination of the work of the new professional curriculum makers and the expression of their ideas, one can begin to understand the Zeitgeist in which the curriculum field was born and thereby some of the reasons that reforms took the course that they did. Although each of these particular reformers reflected a certain individuality, they shared certain common ideals and assumptions about the role of schooling and the way the curriculum should function in that regard. To a large extent, these emerging leaders were driven by a kind of moral mission directed toward righting social wrongs as they saw it and promoting what they felt were the true principles of American democracy as well as the tenets of their Protestant morality.

No single reformer of the period exemplifies the dominant ideology of the curriculum field at the time better than Thomas Jesse Jones. Although not as well known as some of his like-minded contemporaries, Jones not only became a powerful figure in the creation and development of educational policy for African-Americans; his work extended into the wider national arena, particularly through his efforts to transform the social studies as a school subject. In Jones's social outlook and in his career, one can detect not only the motivations that prompted his reform efforts but the ways in which the actual effects of those well-meaning policies sometimes went unrecognized and undetected.

In a burst of indignation, W. E. B. Du Bois once proclaimed Thomas Jesse Jones to be "that evil genius of the Negro race." Whether Jones was in fact a genius or, for that matter, evil, is open to debate; but one thing is certain: Jones was White.[1] Du Bois was objecting to the fact that a position of commanding leadership in African-American affairs was being occupied by a White man; but, perhaps more important, he also was bitterly opposed to the course Jones was steering in terms of educational policy. In particular, Du Bois objected to Jones's emphasis on a curriculum that featured allegedly practical activities and vocational education to the detriment of courses designed to develop the intellect. While Du Bois believed that integration of these two aspects of the curriculum might be theoretically possible, in practice, one was being introduced at the expense of the other. From what he could tell, "the emphasis, and the inspection has to do mainly with the *industrial work as such*, and nobody knows or cares about the chief work for which the school ought to exist." The result was a curriculum designed for future "servants and laborers and *not* educated men and women" (emphasis in original).[2] The implausibility of Jones's leadership role in relation to his background is reflected in a certain ambiguity as to his message and to the legacy of his work. Beyond the course of action he specifically advocated for the education of African-Americans, Jones embodied the ironies and contradictions that were part and parcel of educational reform generally from the turn of the twentieth century onward. The quintessential do-gooder, Jones embarked on what amounted to a mission to African-Americans and succeeded in making himself, to Du Bois's dismay, one of the most important policy makers in the arena of Black education. But his vision was ultimately to transcend the immediate locus of the education of African-Americans; it became the prevailing doctrine for American education generally. Over the course of his career, Jones came to personify at one and the same time the humanitarian zeal, the supreme faith in science, and the emerging professionalism that were inherent in what came to be called progressive education.   *Up ke-*.

Jones was born in Llanfachraeth, Wales, in 1873, the son of a blacksmith. After emigrating to the United States in 1884 with his widowed mother, he pursued his higher education first at Washington and Lee University in Virginia and then at Marietta College in Ohio, where he received his bachelor's degree in 1897. Later, he undertook graduate studies at Columbia University, receiving a Master of Arts degree in 1899 after completing a thesis entitled "Social Phases of Education in the Elementary Schools." He also studied theology at Union Seminary in New York and was awarded a Bachelor of Divinity degree in 1900. Drawn to settlement and charity work, Jones became acting headworker of the University Settlement in New York and at various times worked briefly for the New York Charity Organization Society and the Federation of Churches of New York City. (David Snedden, one of the earliest and most influential of the new breed of educational sociologists, received his doctorate at Columbia University under Edward T. Devine, who was also executive officer of the New York Charity Organization Society.) In addition, Jones was employed briefly by the U.S. Census Bureau. At about the same time, he served as the principal of an elementary school in New York City and as a teacher of economics and history in a secondary school.

The year 1900 marked a turning point in Jones's career. At the age of 27, he was the recipient of the fellowship in sociology at Columbia University and began his Ph.D. studies there under Franklin Giddings, who was to become one of the major forces in American sociology in the twentieth century. Even before he was awarded the fellowship, Jones launched what amounted to a pioneering case study of an urban community in the heart of New York City. Beginning in 1897, he pursued an ambitious study of the residents of a single block on the Upper East Side of Manhattan between Second and Third Avenues. Although the exact street is not recorded, it is probably close to 110th Street in what is now called East Harlem. Both Second Avenue and Third Avenue had elevated train lines which framed the block, and the neighborhood was an overcrowded and dilapidated refuge for mainly Jewish and Italian immigrants, a small step up from the Lower East Side.

SOCIOLOGICAL STUDY OF URBAN IMMIGRANTS

Jones's ideas on education spanned and in a sense integrated two major reform thrusts. The first was the movement that came to be called social gospel. Early in the nineteenth century, organized Protestantism began to turn away from notions of individual guilt and depravity and turned instead to the improvement of the conditions of life as a source of salvation. It was through social melioration rather than individual redemption that souls could be saved. The abolitionist movement in the United States and even the creation of the Salvation Army in England can be traced in part to the influence of this shift in Protestant theology. The second thrust was the application of science to human affairs. Increasingly, the social sciences and sociology in particular were being seen as major forces in the ordering and improvement of the conditions of life. A puzzling and impersonal industrial social order seemed to require the beacon of science to make it work, and it was the new science of society that seemed to offer the greatest promise.

It is in this sense that Jones's Ph.D. sociological research at Columbia University foreshadowed a career that combined a missionary fervor for the uplift of the masses with the language of the new science of society. That new science promised to employ potent new weapons in the cause of social welfare. For his dissertation, entitled "The Sociology of a New York City Block,"[3] Jones concentrated on what he thought to be one of the pressing problems of immigrant life in New York City, the conflict between Jews and Italians. Perceiving that conflict as paralleling the earlier friction between Irish and German immigrants, Jones interviewed hundreds of residents of the tenements he found on "Block X." With remarkable insight, he conceived of the residents of his block as members of urban communities based not solely on geography but on ethnic, religious, and national ties. Since the residents of the 14 apartment buildings he studied were not of one ethnic group, Block X did not in itself constitute one community but consisted instead of enclaves bound to larger ethnically defined communities. Thus, "the five Italian houses in this block form one segment of the large settlement of Italians across Second Avenue," and house 201 became for Jones an Irish village belonging to the county that runs along Third Avenue.[4]

Jones's intermittent experience with charitable organizations and as a census taker, as well as his dark complexion, apparently served him in good stead during his investigation. In the course of his survey, he used forms supplied by the Federation of Churches and was able to gain entry into the homes of his subjects by announcing that he was taking a sociological census and emphasizing the word *census*, thus implying that he was on governmental business. In addition, he reported that he was sometimes taken to be Jewish or Italian, a confusion he actively encouraged. As a result of his divinity studies, for example, he knew some Hebrew, and his rudimentary German was of some use in communicating with his Jewish subjects. (Jones erroneously believed that Jews spoke German.[5] He thought that this gave them an advantage over other immigrants, since he was convinced that, next to English, German was the most important medium of communication in New York City.) He found Italians to be difficult to win over but felt that his dark complexion was to his advantage in gaining their confidence. Since the Irish "fear no one," there was no particular problem in gaining entry into their homes, and, in this case, he could always claim to be "a brother Celt."[6]

Block X included 14 five-story tenements, each floor occupied by four families. Jones's sympathy for the residents of these slums is evident from the outset. He commented on the overcrowding, the lack of proper ventilation and bathroom facilities, and the danger of fire; but he was also self-consciously sociological in his methodology and orientation, reporting figures for density, aggregation, migration, nationality, age, and sex. His social scientific orientation was drawn specifically from an early book by Giddings, *Inductive Sociology,* which concentrated in large measure on the particular ethnic and racial characteristics of various national groups and included an overwhelming reliance on what came to be called connectionist psychology. Italians, for example, were reported by Jones to exhibit a particular "intensity of response to stimulus," in contrast to the superiority of the Anglo-Saxon race as demonstrated in their "close correspondence of stimulus and response."[7] Anglo-Saxons, in other words, reacted appropriately to their environment, whereas Italians overreacted.

Although Jones recognized that nationality alone represented only uncertain evidence and that behavior was affected by living conditions as well as length of residence in the country, he regarded nationality as important in terms of potential responsiveness. A good part of his house-by-house analysis of the residents of Block X, then, consisted of sorting out the characteristics of the various residents in relation to their nationality. Clearly, some of these characteristics were undesirable, but, overall, Jones's prognosis was optimistic. Basically, he felt that as these immigrants spent time in their new country, the beneficial effects of stimuli from their environment would "produce results. . . . The Italian will become less impulsive in his responses and the German less phlegmatic."[8]

To a large extent, Jones's sociological approach involved creating a hierarchy of responses or characteristics and then determining where each of the national groups he studied stood with respect to that hierarchy. For example, he conceived of what he called "methods of appreciation" in terms of four stages in an "ascending series": The first was just an instinctive response to stimuli; the second occurred when the individual not only displayed interest in his or her environment but began to want to know more, thus reaching the stage of "curious inspection"; the third was the state of preferential attention where general interest became specific; and the final and highest state was achieved when the individual not only was curious about the world but reached conclusions after critical inspection.

As a result of his investigation, Jones found for 86 families on Block X, "instinctive response to stimulus . . . to be the dominant method of appreciation," and for an additional 93 families, instinctive response to be "an important subordinate method."[9] When it came to delineating the trait of curiosity by nationality, Jones discovered that, although Italians and Jews both exhibited the characteristic of "curious inspection," they did so in different ways and that this was not necessarily related to emotionality. The Irish, he pointed out, were an emotional people, "but they are heedless as to what is going on about them." The Italians' curiosity was concentrated largely in the area of "law-breaking, prompted by the desire to see how far they can go in this land of the free." Jews, by contrast, exhibited their curiosity particularly in response to questions. When confronted by a questioner, they were likely to respond suspiciously, "For vat you vant to know?"[10] In similar manner, Jones proceeded to classify his subjects with respect to such characteristics as courage, magnanimity, generosity, industriousness, frugality, cleanliness, temperance, truthfulness, and compassion.

Drawing again from *Inductive Sociology*, Jones used Giddings's classificatory scheme of four mental types, ranging from Ideo-Motor, through Ideo-Emotional, to Dogmatic-Emotional, and finally to the highest type, Critically-Intellectual.[11] His subjects' classification by nationality depended on such factors as the way they received him as a visitor and their methods of controlling their children, as well as testimony from informants, such as fire fighters and bill collectors, as to the traits that the various ethnic groups exhibited. Jones also noted that religious affiliation appeared to be on the decline, with Jews and Germans turning to "dogmatic and irrational socialist schemes," while Italians showed a propensity for anarchism. In the end, 38 families, mostly Italians and Irish, turned out to be of the Ideo-Motor type; 170 families were in the Ideo-Emotional category (as well as individuals from 33 other families); six families, mostly Jewish, were Dogmatic-Emotional, as were individuals from 84 other families; and not one family could "with certainty" be classified as Critically-Intellectual.[12]

Obviously, these immigrants had a long way to go, but Jones remained resolute in his determination to accelerate their progress. He concluded his study with a ringing declaration that echoes the social gospel of the nineteenth century in the context of the new social science of the twentieth:

[handwritten marginalia: his opinion/interpretation was that it was suspicious]

[handwritten: Blatant Colonialism and Assimilation]

Every possible agency should be used to change the numerous foreign types into the Anglo-Saxon ideal. The impulsiveness of the Italian must be curbed. The extreme individualism of the Jew must be modified. The shiftlessness of the Irish must give way to perseverance and frugality. And all must be shown the value of the spiritual life.[13]

While the characteristics of his subjects left much to be desired, Jones did not regard those characteristics as fixed or innate. In a true missionary spirit, Jones felt that the unworthy traits of these immigrants could be transmuted in the proper circumstances. *[handwritten: to whom?]*

The chief instrument in this conversion was to be education, and Jones gave some indication as to how sociological expertise could be enlisted in the interest of educational reform. The problem with the existing education was that "all are educated the same." The particular characteristics that the various groups exhibited were simply not taken into account. Thus, "the nervous, flitting, little Italian" was given the same education as "the steady, persevering, plodding little Jew."[14] (Apparently, the only characteristic the two groups had in common was their physical stature.) The new science of sociology provided reformers like Jones with an authoritative basis for pursuing an educational policy based on racial and ethnic typologies.[15] For the time being at least, Jones turned his ministry to the education of African-Americans.

THE NEW SOCIAL STUDIES AT HAMPTON INSTITUTE

A year before he completed his Ph.D. dissertation, Jones became head of the Department of Sociology and History at Hampton Institute and a part-time chaplain. Founded as a normal school in 1868 by a White Yankee industrialist, Samuel Chapman Armstrong, Hampton had developed an emphasis on manual training for its African-American and American Indian students. Manual labor at Hampton was perceived not so much as specific vocational training but as a vehicle for moral regeneration. Honest toil would bring the Protestant ethic to southern Blacks and thus convert them into responsible citizens. Such an ethos was ideal for a man of Jones's temperament and convictions. *[handwritten: Yikes]*

Not only had the curriculum of the Hampton Institute been influenced by a long tradition of providing a distinctly practical education for African-Americans; Armstrong also had been strongly committed to the kind of moral uplift that Jones had made a cornerstone of his mission. In fact, the preeminence of manual training in the curriculum at Hampton was undoubtedly a by-product of the assumed connection between hand labor and moral rehabilitation. It was these curricular practices that brought W. E. B. Du Bois into a spirited disagreement with Hampton's most distinguished graduate and the founder of Tuskegee Institute, Booker T. Washington, and evoked his much more vehement opposition to Jones's educational reforms, eventually challenging the "evil genius's" position of leadership in educational policy making for African-Americans. Du Bois's misgivings were based not on any opposition to achieving economic independence for African-Americans or to moral education generally, but largely on his belief that the kind of manual training that was being provided at institutions like Hampton overemphasized a preindustrial form of hand labor (like basket weaving), which offered little economic benefit in a modern industrial society. Moreover, the dubious promise of economic success was being promoted at the expense of the kind of intellectual education that Du Bois felt was most likely to create a cadre of Black leaders who would promote racial justice. The problem, however, was not simply the prominence of manual training in the curriculum; it extended to the way the other subjects were taught.

Shortly after his arrival at Hampton, Jones embarked on an ambitious effort to transform the lives of the students in his charge through a reconstruction of the social studies as a school subject. Rather than the academic study of history or the social sciences, he conceived of the social studies as addressing directly the problems faced by his students and by society at large. Jones was always careful to delineate the sources of the problems of people of color. They were not the result of inherent deficiencies but the product of historical circumstances and an evolutionary lag and were therefore remediable through education. Both "the Negro and the Indian," he argued, had "little opportunity to understand the essentials of a good home, the duties and responsibilities of citizenship, the cost and meaning of a good education, the place of labor, and the importance of thrift." During the slavery period, for example, only house servants were able to observe the home life of White families and, therefore, the majority were unable to profit from their association with Whites.[16]

A new social studies, including civics, economics, and sociology, could remedy such deficiencies. In the case of civics, Jones sought to address the perception on the part of both the Negro and the Indian that the government was merely "an arbitrary power" and the "feeling of hopelessness" that derives from such a belief. While acknowledging that some legislation did in fact result from prejudice, he sought to convey the idea that such practices were simply the result of evolutionary forces on their way to the development of a true democracy. Like Giddings, Jones believed fervently in "the slow but certain evolutionary progress of government and of society"; that is, what began as matronymic kinship would evolve to patronymic kinship and then on through subsequent stages, "ending in democracy." Two-thirds of the civics course was devoted to the topic of public welfare. In particular, governmental reports were studied in an apparent effort to enlighten Hampton's students in such matters as diet and hygiene. By contrast, Jones regarded the section of the civics course devoted to "the machinery of government" to be "the least important."[17]

The economics course concentrated on wise consumption of goods. Jones was concerned, for example, about "the Negro's preference for ham instead of beef, for fats and sweets instead of nutritive foods, for fancy and brilliantly colored garments instead of the more substantially made clothes." Indian students were encouraged to substitute cattle for ponies on their farms and to acquire the habit of thrift and saving. In general, there was a strong emphasis on various savings institutions, particularly on land institutions that encouraged land ownership. Jones was convinced that "as a farmer owning his land the colored man suffers less from prejudice of those who do not like him than he does in any other occupation."[18]

The main feature of these components of the new social studies was their emphasis on direct functional utility—social welfare in the case of civics and material welfare in the case of economics; but the course in sociology at Hampton had a different emphasis. Here Jones reverted to his own study of sociology and to the "differences in the dispositions" of various groups as well as "in [their] mental and moral characteristics." As such, it should not be surprising that "the [sociology] course at Hampton [was] based upon the outlines and publications of Professor Franklin H. Giddings," with his *Elements of Sociology* used as a textbook. In the section of the course on the "social mind," for example, the fourfold classification of "types of mind" ranging from Ideo-Motor to Critically-Intellectual, which had been a major component of Jones's New York study, was introduced. In this context, Jones sought to convey the sociological "laws" that govern social behavior. In one example drawn from his experience at Hampton, he reported, "One night when the light in a large dining room went out, the least self-controlled of the people in the room began to throw bread crumbs around the dining room." To Jones, this was obviously an instance of the scientific law that states, "Impulsive social action is commenced by those elements of the population that are least controlled." Other sociological laws such as, "Impulsive social action varies inversely with the habit of attaining ends by indirect and complex means," and "Tradition is authoritative and coercive in proportion to its antiquity," were similarly illustrated in the behavior of the Hampton students.[19]

The significance of Jones's use of Giddings's work first as the framework for his Ph.D. dissertation and then as the basis for what became the sociology course at Hampton goes beyond the fact that Jones was Giddings's graduate student. The son of a clergyman, Giddings was instrumental in the emergence of what amounted to a new conception of social science and its role in human affairs. It was this new conception that framed the way a new social studies would be initiated by Jones first at Hampton and then in the country generally. Giddings's professional standing emerged in the context of what Dorothy Ross described as "a growing reformist 'social science' of experts in charities and corrections and of social gospel ministers addressing the 'social question.'"[20] A disciple of Herbert Spencer, Giddings believed that moral and social regeneration could be achieved not through direct intervention but by revealing scientific laws, particularly economic laws, as ex-

[handwritten marginal note: according to Anglo-Saxon writtenness]

hibited by the most advanced practitioners in society. Revelation of the laws themselves, in other words, would preclude the necessity for passionate exhortation or governmental action. Education, of course, could become a powerful instrument for disseminating the best practices in relation to the inadequacies that the students exhibited.

The new social studies at Hampton combined two ingredients that were to become part of what later came to be regarded as pedagogical and social progressivism. In the first, as represented by the courses in civics and economics, academic study was downgraded in favor of directly addressing the problems faced by the students at Hampton. The moral and social deficiencies of the students were identified, and the subject matter was attuned to those deficiencies. In the second, as represented by the course in sociology, the light of science would be brought to bear on the moral and social problems that society faced. In general, the newly emerging social sciences were being enlisted in the cause of social melioration. With remarkable energy and ingenuity, Jones was able to mobilize his messianic impulses in the cause of rehabilitating the downtrodden through what amounted to curriculum reform, particularly in the social studies. At the same time, of course, he also was enhancing his own status as a social scientist and a professional educator.

THE HAMPTON SOCIAL STUDIES AS A MODEL FOR THE NATION

Had Jones's new social studies been confined to the Hampton Institute alone, it would still constitute a revealing chapter in the development of African-American education in the United States. Largely through Jones's own efforts, however, the new social studies began to take on national prominence as well.[21] The principal vehicle for conveying Jones's version of the social studies as a school subject to the nation at large was the Commission on the Reorganization of Secondary Education. Under the sponsorship of the National Education Association, the report of the Commission, *Cardinal Principles of Secondary Education*, embodied what was considered to be the new conception of education, one tied much more closely to directly functional outcomes than to academic studies. A direct successor to the Committee on High School and College, the Commission was quick to appoint subcommittees whose task was perceived to be the reconstruction of the various subject areas along functional lines. The committee on social studies was created in 1912 with Jones, now an employee of the Bureau of Education, as chairman.[22] Heading the Commission and the guiding force behind the *Cardinal Principles* report as a whole was a kindred spirit, Clarence Darwin Kingsley.

Although Kingsley was of a somewhat higher social class, the main lines of his early life bear a remarkable resemblance to Jones's. Born one year after Jones, in 1874, Kingsley also suffered the loss of his father at an early age. During his undergraduate years at Colgate University, he studied for the Baptist ministry, and upon abandoning his formal theological studies, he turned to social work. After staying on at Colgate for 4 years as a mathematics instructor, he obtained a job with the same New York Charity Organization Society where Jones had been employed for a while. Kingsley worked particularly with homeless men and actually lived in a tenement district not unlike the one that Jones studied. Like Jones, he too undertook graduate work at Columbia University, concentrating in the social sciences, including courses in sociology with Giddings. In 1904, the year Jones completed his Ph.D. dissertation, Kingsley completed his Master of Science degree with a thesis entitled "The Treatment of Homeless Men in New York City."

After becoming somewhat disillusioned with social settlement work, Kingsley turned to education as the outlet for his humanitarian impulses. In 1904, he became a mathematics teacher at the Manual Training High School in Brooklyn, New York, and by 1913 he had developed the proposal to the National Education Association on the articulation of high school and college that eventuated in the appointment of the Commission on the Reorganization of Secondary Education.

Over the course of his tenure at Manual Training High School, Kingsley rose to a leadership position in the High School Teachers Association and, as a member of the Committee on Revision of the Course of Study, worked to reconstruct the course of study around life activities. Both Giddings and Snedden were invited to address the Association during this period, with Giddings taking the occasion to declare, "High school education should make citizens not learners," and Snedden arguing in favor of adapting the curriculum to the six types of students he had identified.[23] Three years after becoming commissioner of education in Massachusetts in 1909, Snedden designated Kingsley as the agent for high schools. Clearly, however, the apex of Kingsley's career was his appointment to chair the Commission on the Reorganization of Secondary Education, and it was this appointment that permitted him to extend his mission from the confines of New York City and later Massachusetts to the country at large. The relationship between his religious evangelism and his work in education was not lost on Kingsley himself. In a letter to his mother a year before he died at the age of 52, Kingsley alluded to the fact that the reports of his Commission were being used in China. "So you see your little boy," he wrote, "while he did not go as a missionary to China, has written something that may be of real help to that great people in building a new educational system to meet the needs of a better type of living."[24]

Kingsley's work in giving leadership and direction to the *Cardinal Principles* report had long-range effects. For many years after its publication in 1918, the report was regarded as the yardstick against which educational reform could be measured. By the middle of the twentieth century, the practice of producing lists of the goals of schooling on the model of Kingsley's famous seven aims became a cottage industry. (Every one of the 50 states and many foreign countries have produced an official list of aims.) The list of aims that Kingsley produced was one of the instruments used to redirect school subjects along directly functional lines. Subjects that could not demonstrate their efficacy in achieving such aims as worthy use of leisure, citizenship, worthy home membership, vocation, and ethical character needed to be cast out of the curriculum.[25]

As chairman of the committee on social studies, Jones played a role in creating a new social studies that was scrupulously consistent with the overall thrust of the *Cardinal Principles* report and one of the most influential. In fact, historian Edward A. Krug argued that Jones's committee was among the most successful efforts of the entire enterprise.[26] This should not be surprising. The *Cardinal Principles* report as a whole essentially endorsed a curriculum tied directly to the social functions that future citizens would perform. What could be more effective in that undertaking than a reconstructed social studies as a school subject? But to be successful, the grip of academic study (usually associated with preparation for college) had to be loosened.

Jones's 1913 preliminary report on the social studies committee is actually more revealing than the 1916 final report. Here, Jones was able to give free reign to the new direction he envisioned for American education generally and for the social studies in particular. With respect to civics, for example, he declared that "the old civics, almost exclusively a study of Government machinery, must give way to the new civics, a study of all manner of efforts to improve mankind." Even history "must answer the test of good citizenship."[27] Clearly, however, civics was the centerpiece of the new social studies, and in that regard Jones followed the main lines of the new social studies he had developed at Hampton. "Fully two-thirds" of civics, for example, should be devoted to the relationship between government and public welfare, with attention being given to the work of nongovernmental agencies whose mission is social melioration. Specific topics included pure food and milk, waste disposal, and "health crusades."[28] Like the new social studies that he created at Hampton, then, the new social studies being recommended for all schools combined social uplift and social science, with correspondingly less emphasis on the academic study of history. *no wonder*

The final report of the social studies committee, "compiled" under its secretary, Arthur William Dunn, was somewhat muted by comparison, but its major thrust was still clear. Declaring at the outset that "the keynote of modern education is 'social efficiency,' and [that] all subjects should contribute to this end,"[29] the committee report went on to emphasize the special role a new social studies would play in that regard. The ideal of social efficiency, which was to dominate educational thinking for most of the twentieth century, is perhaps best epitomized by Frederick Winslow Taylor's scientific management in industry.[30] It combined

Process or state of improvement

Native American narrative/voice disappeared from "history"

moral uplift with the hard realities of a science defined in terms of precision and predictability. The great appeal of social efficiency lay in its promise of a stable and balanced social order that could run as efficiently as a modern factory. Just as the modern factory assigned a place and specific function for each worker, so society would perform best when each citizen was trained specifically and directly for his or her place in the social order. In a time of rapid social change, that vision was an extraordinarily powerful one.

For the most part, the subcommittee report consisted of a plan to reorganize secondary social studies into two "cycles": The junior cycle, grades 7–9, would consist of geography, European history, American history, and civics; and the senior cycle, grades 10–12, would comprise European history, American history, and a course in problems of democracy. In the implementation of such a plan, however, the subcommittee emphasized what it called "differentiation of courses."[31] Thus, it seemed likely to the subcommittee members that the children of immigrants would need more American history and less European history than native-born Americans. Although Kingsley's basic moderation precluded actually casting out academic subjects such as history, the report clearly leaned in the direction of subjects that promised direct functional utility, such as community civics. In fact, the report noted that an objection had been raised as to the great amount of civics being recommended in grades 7–11 and sought to justify such an allocation.[32]

The *Cardinal Principles* report has been accurately called "an archeological deposit of many ideas and influences,"[33] but the ideas that emerged as the most influential in terms of actual practice were those tied most closely to the theme of social efficiency and the consequent downgrading of academic study in the American curriculum. While the recommendations of the Commission on the Reorganization of Secondary Education did not restrict the so-called academic subjects as much as some social efficiency reformers, such as Snedden, would have wished, subjects like English, history, and mathematics clearly had to reorient themselves along functional lines, defined by the list of seven aims. To a large extent, this was prompted by humanitarian impulses and promoted under slogans like "meeting the needs and interests of students" by attending to the particular characteristics and defects they exhibited. This was, of course, what Jones had been promoting all along.

RESIDUE OF JONES'S EDUCATIONAL POLICY

In many ways, Jones was the model of the new education professional. He was in no sense a genius, but he very much embodied and exemplified what educational reform was to become in the twentieth century and thus provides a vehicle for reexamining the direction that much educational reform was taking. In particular, he combined humanitarian zeal with the certainty of science in the interest of a conception of education that was to dominate reform efforts in what most people would regard as the progressive era. But, in adopting this stance, Jones and his ideological compatriots also were perpetuating an inferior political status for the very clients they were seeking to elevate. For one thing, the language of social science that the new class of professionals employed relegated their clients to subservience while enhancing their own status. Much in the manner of some missionaries, they knew with near certainty what was wrong with their benighted and backward clientele, and they set about correcting those deficiencies. With respect to the helping professions in general, political theorist Murray Edelman has argued that the language professionals use really perpetuates "a world in which the weak and the wayward need to be controlled for their own good."[34] As a professional reformer, Jones was in a position to define the problems and impose the solutions by virtue of his command of the language of science.

It is professional language, then, that subtly creates a power relationship in which the alleged beneficiaries of a service are placed in a position of subordination. By portraying in scientific terms first immigrants, then African-Americans, and finally Americans generally as somehow deficient in terms of the Anglo-Saxon ideal, Jones inadvertently laid the groundwork for a relatively permanent inequality of power between the professional class he represented and the clients he served with such dedication. Category systems of the sort that Jones borrowed from Giddings, because they were presented as scientifically valid, made their political message all the more compelling. They assigned the objects of their attention to particular niches in a social pecking order and undermined their political potency. It is the professional, after all, who gets to delineate the imperatives that control any situation, and it is the client who must play the role of grateful beneficiary. This is very much the situation that raised Du Bois's hackles in the first place. Who needed a White man to define problems and prescribe solutions for African-Americans?

It is of considerable significance, however, that the impact of the ideology that Jones espoused was not limited to African-Americans. The doctrine that impelled the new social studies reached far beyond its immediate locus. What was conceived of as a social studies for moral regeneration and social uplift rather than for academic excellence in the context of Hampton Institute, in effect made itself felt in the way many Americans conceived of the role of education generally. The common ideological ingredient in the social studies at Hampton and the new social studies as prescribed by the *Cardinal Principles* report is the notion, so perfectly realized in Jones's work, that the social studies and, by extension, education itself exist not for intellectual mastery in the modern world or for enlightened self-interest, but for a restricted conception of moral rectitude and social equilibrium. Education becomes the instrument through which enlightened professional missionaries deliver their urgent social message to the benighted masses. In a sense,

Defect Model

the function of schooling becomes confounded with the function of organizations such as the New York Charity Organization Society.

Beyond the confines of Jones's new social studies, then, lay a broader conception of education seen not as a liberating intellectual force but as a way to achieve social salvation by addressing the specific defects exhibited by the target populations. That policy manifested itself originally in the idea that immigrants needed definite remedial training if they were to progress toward achieving the Anglo-Saxon ideal; then it appeared as an education for African-Americans and American Indians that consisted essentially of making the fruits of the dominant culture available to a backward population; and, finally, it incorporated the social efficiency ideal of using education generally as an instrument for smoothing out the wrinkles in the existing social fabric.

evolving process

Jones, of course, was not the only or even the principal architect of a policy that sought to make a large segment of the population the dutiful recipients of the largesse of social missionaries. He was not in the front rank of educational reformers of his day either in terms of the integrity of his ideas or his national visibility; but he is exquisitely representative of the predominant reform credo of his day and, to an extent, of ours. Given prevailing social and economic forces of Jones's time, the social gospel as well as the primitive social science he preached undoubtedly would have flourished even if his career had taken an entirely different course. Nevertheless, Jones's career becomes a prism through which to view the development of the curriculum in the twentieth century and even some of the forces that drive American educational policy today. If nothing else, his ideology draws attention to the virulent anti-intellectualism that emerged as a by-product of certain lines of educational reform, such as social efficiency.

It would be easy to dismiss merely as quaintly archaic the ideology that lay behind Jones's work in creating a new social studies and, in effect, a new education. The science of society that Giddings propounded and that Jones embraced did, after all, incorporate large elements of social Darwinism, ingenuous do-goodism, and strong doses of racism as well. A larger policy question, however, lurks behind that facade of moral uplift and naive social science. It is whether education as a public enterprise exists *to educate* or for some more explicit and presumably more noble purpose, such as to save souls by attending directly to the particular social and personal needs of the school population. One can always prescribe doing both in schools, but one purpose, as Du Bois noted, does seem to crowd out the other.

There is more than simple irony in the fact that the new social studies designed by Jones for the rehabilitation of African-Americans in the South became the model for social studies for the nation at large. Not only did that conception of the function of social studies extend to the larger population geographically; it ultimately extended beyond the confines of social studies as a school subject to the curriculum as a whole. In fact, many of the prevailing justifications for improving the American educational system are quite consistent with Jones's conception of the function of public education. The current national mood seems to dictate that not only social studies but the curriculum generally must be made the direct instrument of national well-being, with well-being interpreted largely in economic terms. What becomes subordinated in this view is Du Bois's contrasting vision of education in the interest of intellectual independence, along with the enfranchisement and power that intellectual independence can bring.

CHAPTER 3

The *Cardinal Principles* Report
as Archaeological Deposit

One of the signal events in the history of American educational reform is the issuance of the Cardinal Principles *report in 1918 by the National Education Association's Commission on the Reorganization of Secondary Education. To many historians and educators, that report marked the emergence of a new and more functional approach to American education. The report's far-reaching proposals often are contrasted with the much more modest recommendations of the Committee of Ten report, which first appeared in 1893. The earlier committee is widely thought to have ignored the educational significance of rapidly changing social conditions as well as the dramatic shift in both the size and nature of the secondary school population. By contrast, the* Cardinal Principles *report, appearing only 25 years later, commonly is seen as being very much in keeping with the needs of a modern industrial democracy. In a very real sense, the* Cardinal Principles *report, as the title of this essay suggests, is an invaluable collection of the conceptual artifacts of early-twentieth-century education, many of which are still reflected in the contemporary curriculum.*

Critical examination of the Cardinal Principles *report's presuppositions and recommendations provides a revealing picture of the ideological underpinnings of many curriculum reforms, as they were advanced and implemented not just around 1918 but for most of the twentieth century. As this essay indicates, the stodgy academic conservatism that the Committee of Ten report is supposed to illustrate may have in the end represented a more democratic and ultimately a more defensible educational approach to designing a high school curriculum than the seemingly advanced pronouncements of the* Cardinal Principles *report. Similarly, the effort on the part of the Commission on the Reorganization of Secondary Education to promote a much more wide-ranging and differentiated course of study, in order to meet the needs of a diverse school population, may have resulted in a pernicious bifurcation of the curriculum based on the probable destination of students and led to further stratification along social class, racial, and gender lines.*

The appearance of the *Cardinal Principles of Secondary Education* in 1918 marked the culmination of a quarter century of educational policy pronouncements by various committees of the National Education Association (NEA).[1] Beginning with the Committee of Ten report in 1893,[2] with which the *Cardinal Principles* report often is contrasted, the NEA undertook to shape the purposes, course of study, and structure of that newly dominant form of secondary education in the United

States, the high school. It would be difficult to establish that any one of these reports in itself—or even all of them cumulatively—actually molded the American high school into the kind of institution that it has become; but, in Edward Krug's apt characterization, the *Cardinal Principles* report in particular represents an invaluable "archaeological deposit."[3] From the vestiges of that period, we may begin to reconstruct the educational and social ideals that prompted Americans to undertake that most radical of pedagogical experiments, universal secondary education, and perhaps even to find some clues as to what went wrong. Examination of the ideals and doctrines that lay behind that experiment is made all the more timely by the fact that the success of the venture is at present still in doubt. Of the various levels of education—primary, secondary, and tertiary—it is American secondary education that is clearly the most besieged.

THE COMMITTEE OF TEN AND THE *CARDINAL PRINCIPLES* REPORTS CONTRASTED

In a sense, both the Committee of Ten report and the *Cardinal Principles* report have two histories. One, obviously, is the history of the events and ideologies that gave rise to the reports, as well as to whatever impact they may have had; and the second is the history of the interpretations that have been assigned to these reports over the course of the twentieth century. The latter is particularly interesting since the two reports—and particularly the contrast between them—have entered into the mythology that has attended modern educational reform in the United States and has served to legitimate certain kinds of curriculum practices as well as to impugn others. According to the interpretation that has prevailed for most of the twentieth century, the benighted Committee of Ten report failed to consider the full implications of what a system of mass secondary education would entail, whereas the far-sighted *Cardinal Principles* report ushered in the era of truly democratic secondary schools by tying the curriculum to functional outcomes.

That interpretation has been given a certain plausibility by the two men who were mainly responsible for the reports and who, in an important sense, have come to represent two ideological poles. The 1893 report was essentially the work of Charles W. Eliot (1834–1926), distinguished president of Harvard University, whose very appearance, including his mutton chops and stern visage, makes for a convenient symbol of Victorian elitism. By contrast, the guiding force behind the 1918 report was Clarence O. Kingsley, a relatively obscure mathematics teacher from Brooklyn, New York, who had undertaken the reform of American secondary education as a kind of special mission. Given the direction that the secondary school curriculum was to take over the course of the twentieth century, the two committee reports provided American educators with a serviceable way to highlight the old versus the new, the aristocratic versus the democratic.

Lending plausibility to these symbols are the main recommendations of the two reports, which appear on the surface at least to fit neatly into that pattern. The centerpiece of the Committee of Ten report, for example, was a set of four model programs of secondary education, each of which, it was argued by the committee, would serve both as preparation for college and as preparation for "life." Each of those 4-year programs of study—Classical, Latin-Scientific, Modern Languages, and English—was strongly academic in nature, excluding such newly emerging subjects as manual training and commercial courses. All four programs included, for example, 3 years of mathematics and at least 4 years of a foreign language, as well as heavy doses of science and literature. To latter-day interpreters of this recommendation, the four courses of study represented a clear case of colleges imposing a college preparatory curriculum on American secondary schools, and the theme of overcoming college domination of the secondary-school curriculum became a compelling one for many school reformers. In large measure, the persistence of subjects like algebra, chemistry, literature, and foreign languages was perceived to be an artifact of that long-standing college domination. A corollary of that interpretation was that Eliot and his fellow committee members were ignoring the needs and interests of ordinary people and, consciously or subconsciously, were pursuing a course that would perpetuate an elitist educational system.

A second recommendation of the Committee of Ten was at least as controversial and lent further credence to the charge that it favored a select few within the secondary-school population. Eliot had polled the heads of the various subject subcommittees to determine their views on the extent to which there should be different courses of study designed for those preparing for entry into college and for those whose education would not go further than secondary school. Their answer was unanimously in the negative, in essence declining to make a curricular distinction based on probable destination after high school. To critics, this was simply another instance of the committee failing to take into account the realities of the new secondary education, such as the great variation in ability within the high school population. One prominent reformer, for example, renowned psychologist G. Stanley Hall, presented a range of criticisms of the report, accusing the committee in the end of failing to take into account that "great army of incapables" who were then invading the high schools.[4] The emergence of the mental measurement movement in the early decades of the twentieth century lent a kind of credibility to such charges. Tested intelligence in the form of I.Q. scores seemed to support the idea that differences in ability necessitated different courses of study.

It was in the context of such criticisms of the Committee of Ten's recommendations that the *Cardinal Principles* report emerged as a convenient counterpoint. The fact that the NEA chose Kingsley to head the commission is itself significant in this regard. A man of deep religious convictions, Kingsley (1874–1926) once aspired to become a missionary in China. He also was heavily involved in various charitable causes, and his master's degree thesis at Columbia University was a study of homeless men. After becoming a teacher at Manual Training High School in Brooklyn, New York, he quickly rose to a leadership position in the High School Teachers Association and in 1910 was appointed to head the NEA's Committee on the Articulation of High School and College. Having admired that committee's report, David Snedden, then Massachusetts Commissioner of Education, invited Kingsley to accept the position of supervisor of secondary schools in 1912. When the NEA's Commission on the Reorganization of Secondary Education was formed in 1913, Kingsley was appointed to head it.

IMPACT OF SOCIAL CHANGE

Beyond the contrast in the background and personalities of Eliot and Kingsley lay a growing realization on the part of educational and social leaders as well as Americans generally that a profound change had taken place in the nature of American society. The *Cardinal Principles* report opens with an allusion to the fact that "within the past few decades [profound changes] have taken place in American life." Particular attention is drawn to changes in the workplace, "the substitution of the factory system for the domestic system of industry; the use of machinery in the place of manual labor; the high specialization of processes with a corresponding division of labor; and the breakdown of the apprentice system."[5] The implication, of course, is that the social changes to which the report alludes require equally profound changes in the way secondary education should be conceived.

In an essay that, in many respects, captures the tone for interpreting both the Committee of Ten and the *Cardinal Principles* reports, Lawrence Cremin argued that in the period between 1893 and 1918, "political, economic and social changes of the first magnitude were beginning to occasion new demands on the school," and that the Commission on the Reorganization of Secondary Education that Kingsley headed was responding to those demands in a way that the Committee of Ten could not. Cremin pointed first of all to the triumph of industrialism and the movement from hand labor to factory labor. Then, too, there was the problem of mass immigration and, in particular, the shift around 1880 in the immigration pattern from northern and western Europe to southern and eastern Europe. Since the newer immigrants tended to congregate in large cities instead of settling land to the west, new challenges were presented in the area of citizenship education. And finally, there was the emergence of social and political progressivism as a movement that offered the hope of ameliorating social conditions through governmental action such as antimonopoly and child labor laws. These factors, Cremin argued, contributed to a vision of secondary education that was vastly different from that offered by the Committee of Ten.

The changes to which Cremin alluded were real enough, but the way in which people reacted to these social and political transformations was anything but uniform. The responses to these changes in the social fabric not only varied, but were sometimes antagonistic to one another. A case in point was the perceived decline in family influence as a result of industrialization. In an agricultural economy, children tended to work side by side with their parents and other adult family members, and this tended to have a significant socializing effect. In an industrial society, along with its consequent urbanization, parents were often absent from the home for large portions of the day, and this implied a new role for the school.[6]

In 1899, when John Dewey considered the implications of this shift, he undertook to create closer ties between home and school and to infuse into the curriculum of his Laboratory School those fundamental "occupations," like growing food and making clothing, that had given way to the new industrialism. For Dewey, the task was to restore the beneficial influence that families had once exercised.[7] By contrast, Edward A. Ross, in his classic sociological study, *Social Control*, welcomed the decline of parental influence. The state, after all, could exercise little control over who became a parent, whereas teachers were "picked persons," who, with their "rare and splendid personalities," were more likely to exercise a more beneficent influence over the child than a mother or a father would. For Ross, the weakening of the family structure offered a new opportunity for society to have a more direct impact on children's socialization through its schools.[8] There was indeed a perception around the turn of the twentieth century that families were in decline, but the question of what to do about it was filtered through an array of different ideological lenses. The social changes that were becoming increasingly evident around that time did not direct the course of educational and social policy; they provided the occasion for various ideological positions to emerge and to compete for public acceptance and allegiance.

One consequence of industrialization was the emergence of new interest groups that sought to influence American educational policy particularly with respect to the way secondary schools were structured. The National Association of Manufacturers (NAM), for example, was formed in 1896 and within a year was calling for radical changes in American education. In particular, it became a major force for promoting vocational education at public expense. The president of NAM, Theodore C. Search, was an ardent advocate of the German system of secondary education with its differentiated secondary schools, each with a different purpose and designed for a different population. Search and his fellow NAM members expressed concern that the German school system put American manufacturers at a distinct disadvantage in terms of the skills needed in the workplace and hence in an inferior position in terms of world markets.[9]

Sentiment was so strong for emulating the German system of secondary education in the early years of the twentieth century that individual states began to consider taking steps in that direction. In Chicago, the powerful Chicago Association of Commerce, organized in 1904, lent its strong support to the Cooley bill, which was being considered in the Illinois legislature in 1911. Edwin G. Cooley, a former superintendent of Chicago's schools, had toured Europe inspecting vocational education programs there and returned with a plan to create a dual system of education after sixth grade, one offering vocational programs and the other general education. Influential Illinois interest groups such as the Commercial Club, the Illinois Manufacturers' Association, and the Industrial Club supported the bill. In the years leading up to the *Cardinal Principles* report, it was anything but clear that Americans would not adopt the bifurcated system of secondary education that was prevalent in parts of Europe at the time.

The continuing controversy over the Cooley bill prompted the entry of John Dewey into the fray. He questioned the appropriateness of trying to emulate the German system of schooling, referring to it as "frankly nationalistic" and deploring the effort "to turn schools into preliminary factories at public expense."[10] Snedden, an ardent advocate of the dual system, was dismayed by Dewey's attack and took issue with his position that the proposed new system would be "beneficial chiefly to employers." He went on to argue that the matter of whether to institute a separate system of vocational education at the secondary-school level was not a matter of particular pedagogical significance; rather it was "merely one of securing the greatest efficiency."[11] In his reply, Dewey condemned the effort to provide a "bookish" education for one group of secondary-school students and narrow skill training for the other. For Dewey, the issue was not even "so much narrowly educational but profoundly political and social." Deploring the effort to adapt future workers to the existing industrial system, he added pointedly, "I am not sufficiently in love with the regime for that."[12] The differences in how to interpret a major social upheaval like industrialization in terms of educational policy were contentious and far-reaching.

THE *CARDINAL PRINCIPLES* REPORT'S RESPONSE TO SOCIAL CHANGE

It was in the context of these debates over the role and function of secondary education in the United States that the *Cardinal Principles* report was born. While Kingsley had been, in a sense, Snedden's protege, he tended to be more moderate in the way he interpreted the new realities of the industrial society. That moderation is reflected in the commission's recommendation that the comprehensive high school rather than specialized high schools become the setting for American secondary education. In that respect, Kingsley can be seen as carrying forward Horace Mann's nineteenth-century ideal of a system of common (elementary) schools in which students of all social classes would mingle together in public schools and ultimately form common bonds, thereby minimizing invidious distinctions with respect to wealth and privilege. At the same time, however, Kingsley's report sought to reflect the needs of an industrial society through a differentiated curriculum. The model institution of secondary education in the United States would be the comprehensive high school, but a differentiated curriculum would attend to the allegedly significant differences in ability as well as the multifarious needs of an industrial democracy.

In the context of the times, the authors of the *Cardinal Principles* report could hardly afford to ignore the evidence being brought forth by some psychologists that there was indeed wide variation in ability among people, nor could they fail to notice that the secondary-school population was beginning to grow dramatically. In 1890, for example, only 6.7% of adolescents between 14 and 17 were attending public or private high schools. By 1920, 2 years after the *Cardinal Principles* report was issued, that figure had reached 32.4%. Over those critical 3 decades, the secondary-school population had grown more than fourfold. Given that growth, combined with the new emphasis on variation in human ability, the commission tried to come to terms with the prospect that the growth in American secondary education could not be interpreted simply in terms of sheer numbers, but had to be considered in terms of a wider spread in the ability of secondary-school students and hence in their destinations within the social order.

It was primarily for this reason that the *Cardinal Principles* commission chose to depart from the pattern advocated by the Committee of Ten and to recommend instead that "differentiated curriculums" be devised in terms of vocation. Specifically mentioned are "agricultural, business, clerical, industrial, fine-arts, and household-arts curriculums."[13] Unlike the four programs recommended by the Committee of Ten, the types of curriculum recommended by Kingsley's commission sought to match courses of study with the probable destinations or classifications of secondary-school students. The idea that such a course of action was consistent with principles of American democracy, particularly in terms of equality of educational opportunity, became an abiding article of faith for most of the twentieth century. To do otherwise, it was frequently argued, would be to favor an academic elite over the interests of the new population of secondary-school students. To this day, proponents of "tech-prep," a popular plan to divide the high school population into three distinct groups, each with a curriculum attuned to a different social and occupational destiny, decry the emphasis on academic subjects as preferring a select segment of the high school population. Even the commonly used terms "college-entrance student" and "college-entrance subject," as well as their "noncollege-entrance" counterparts, reflect, strictly speaking, not academic ability but probable destination. In a subtle way, therefore, the *Cardinal Principles* commission's concern for adjusting the curriculum to different ability levels was transformed into a form of social predestination.

The tendency to see education, particularly secondary education, in terms of future adult roles is, of course, consistent with the prevailing doctrine of social efficiency as enunciated by the likes of Snedden, Kingsley's mentor. One key element of social efficiency doctrine was to teach future citizens only those things that they needed in order to function effectively as adult members of society. Anything beyond that would be wasteful. Inevitably, this involved predicting one's future place in the social order and adapting the curriculum to the demands dictated by that social role. Liberal education would be no less functional than vocational education. According to Snedden, "[v]ocational education is designed to make a person an efficient producer; liberal education may be designed to make him an efficient consumer or user."[14] To be sure, Kingsley's commitment to social efficiency was more subdued than Snedden's, but it was there nevertheless and it strongly influenced the way in which the recommendations of the *Cardinal Principles* report were constructed. The new secondary education would be democratic, of course, but a democratic education still meant, in Kingsley's mind, shaping the individual to find his or her niche in the social order as a way making that social order operate more efficiently. "[E]ducation in a democracy," the report declares, "should develop in each individual the knowledge, interests, ideals, habits, and powers whereby he will find his or her place and use that place to shape both himself and society to ever nobler ends."[15] Typically, the language is moderate, but the message is still clear.

THE SEVEN AIMS OF SECONDARY EDUCATION

The impact of social efficiency doctrine is also evident in what is by far the most well-known section of the *Cardinal Principles* report, its statement of the seven aims of secondary education. In contrast to the implied aim of secondary education embedded in the Committee of Ten report—intellectual development—the 1918 report listed (1) health, (2) command of fundamental processes, (3) worthy home-membership, (4) vocation, (5) citizenship, (6) worthy use of leisure, and finally (7) ethical character, as the governing purposes of secondary education.[16] For many years after the report was issued, these aims were cited as the highest wisdom in defining the curriculum of secondary education, and commentary on the aims took the form not so much of examining their implications with respect to curriculum design but of decrying the slow pace of progress in realizing them.

Whether the enunciation of these seven aims actually precipitated the enormous expansion of the scope of secondary-school curriculum over the course of the twentieth century or whether the aims merely reflected a direction that would have been carried forward anyway is almost beside the point. (It was probably the latter.) Of critical importance, however, is what those aims came to symbolize in terms of how the secondary-school curriculum should be conceived. One of the abiding legacies of the *Cardinal Principles* report is its symbolic shift from an education conceived as the development of the intellect to an education conceived as directly utilitarian in terms of the lives of future citizens. Although Kingsley stopped short of recommending the abandonment of academic subjects for all but a segment of the high school population (as Snedden would have preferred), his sympathies unquestionably lay with a curriculum that functioned directly in a wide variety of activities that human beings are called upon to perform. This would be accomplished not so much by eliminating academic subjects or even subordinating them to practical subjects, but by reconstructing them along functional lines so that they could be made to address at least one of the seven aims. In this way, Kingsley hoped not only to make the new high school curriculum more relevant to the lives of the new population of secondary-school students, but also to have it contribute directly to a stable and smoothly running social order.

Sometimes overlooked in discussions of the implications of the *Cardinal Principles* report is the fact the main report was supplemented by several subcommittee reports on different subject areas (as was the case with the Committee of Ten report). It is the transformation of some school subjects, not their displacement or abandonment, that may be the most concrete manifestation of the report's recommendations. Although the terminology with regard to school subjects may have undergone some modification over the years, it is the less visible changes wrought under the familiar subject labels that are among the most significant modifications in the American secondary-school curriculum in the more than three-quarters of a century since the report was issued. In one sense, the school subjects survived the onslaught by social efficiency educators; but the nature of the subjects—what is taught under the labels of English, social studies, mathematics, and the like—has undergone considerable change.

More than anything, however, the widely admired seven aims of the *Cardinal Principles* report gave secondary schools license to expand the curriculum almost indefinitely. With the exception of "command of fundamental processes" (by which was meant, oddly enough, reading, writing, and arithmetic), the remaining six are not so much aims to be achieved as categories of living. Almost no activity that human beings engage in could not be subsumed under one of those categories. Thus, almost anything that the human imagination could conceive of became fodder for the secondary-school curriculum. The teaching of poetry could be justified (improbably) in terms of "worthy use of leisure," but baking a cherry pie also could be legitimated as somehow contributing to "worthy home-membership." By conceiving of the aims of secondary education in such broad terms, Kingsley was able to appease warring parties and allay certain fears with respect to the effects of social change. The fundamental weakness of the seven aims, however, is that they exclude practically nothing, and, in fact, one of the most critical problems that American secondary education faces today is the profound absence of purpose, cohesion, and direction caused in part by the uncontrolled proliferation of school subjects. Kingsley's moderation had its costs.

AFTERMATH OF THE COMMISSION'S RECOMMENDATIONS

Jeffrey Mirel and David Angus have analyzed the effects of the expansion of the American high school curriculum over the course of the twentieth century in terms of equality of educational opportunity.[17] They found that between 1922 (4 years after the *Cardinal Principles* report) and 1973, the sheer number of discrete courses offered in American high schools increased from approximately 175 to more than 2,100. In addition, from roughly 1930 to 1970, the number of high school students taking academic courses declined steadily. Since 1970, under the influence of the so-called "excellence" reforms, a reversal of that trend has begun to be felt. Mirel and Angus argue that "what occurred from the 1920s to the 1970s was the steady triumph of the philosophy embodied in *Cardinal Principles*."[18] As it turns out, the effort to broaden the curriculum to include "personal development" courses has had an unequal impact on Black and working-class youth as they began to attend secondary schools in much greater numbers. Mirel and Angus conclude that "*equal educational opportunity was not achieved by lowering academic standards through curricular differentiation, tracking, shortening courses from two semesters to one, and giving academic credit to previously extracurricular activities.*"[19] If we take the intent of the *Cardinal Principles* report to be promoting equal educational opportunity in the face of the reality of mass secondary education, then it appears that the policy of "dumbing down" the curriculum simply has not worked.

In retrospect, the failure of that policy raises the question of whether the Committee of Ten's recommendation of providing an academic education for all, regardless of probable destination, is so elitist after all. Putting all youth in touch with the intellectual resources of their culture may, in the end, be a more democratic policy than providing high-status knowledge for some and low-status knowledge for the rest. But it would be a mistake to assume that a return to "the good old days" will somehow address the problem. The fact is that there were no good old days. If the ideal of an academic education for all is to be achieved, the subjects that traditionally constitute the secondary-school curriculum will need to be reconstructed and interrelationships among those subjects will need to be recognized or invented. If the subjects that constitute a common curriculum are to be organized around the goal of intellectual development rather than the potpourri of aims that frame the curriculum advanced by the *Cardinal Principles* report, then it becomes all the more important to rethink what an intellectual command of the modern world really entails. It may, for example, entail a breaking down of traditional subject-matter boundaries and a corresponding integration of subjects that traditionally have been kept apart, much as what takes place on the frontiers of scholarship. That integration also could be extended to integrating traditional academic subjects with the world of everyday reality so that disciplined intelligence can be brought to bear on real problems.

change for NOW

To be sure, the *Cardinal Principles* report embodied the reform impulse that has dominated thinking with respect to curriculum policy, but, in its recommendations, it went much too far in the direction of rejecting, or at least depreciating, the value of an academic education. The indefinite expansion of the American secondary curriculum, including the substitution of "personal development" courses for academic ones, over the course of the twentieth century is not really a direct outgrowth of the enunciation of the seven aims; it is merely consistent with it. Given the prevailing ideologies, it is likely that secondary education would have followed roughly the same pattern even without those aims. The significance of the seven aims lies not in the fact that they actually directed the course of American secondary education; but they do represent one highly suggestive pottery shard in the "archaeological deposit" we call the *Cardinal Principles* report. From artifacts such as those aims, we can begin to reconstruct the prevailing attitudes and doctrines that helped fashion the contours of the modern secondary-school curriculum. That done, we may even be able to take the kind of corrective action that will help put future generations in command of those intellectual tools that will permit them to gain some measure of control over their lives and fortunes.

CHAPTER 4

A Century of Growing Antagonism
in High School–College Relations

In the minds of many school reformers, true curriculum reform has been thwarted largely through the baleful influence of the colleges, especially affecting secondary schools. By insisting on a particular pattern of preparation for college, so the argument goes, colleges have served to perpetuate a curriculum organized around traditional disciplines of knowledge, and thereby the colleges have had a fatally inhibiting effect on curriculum experimentation. Terms like "college-entrance curriculum" and "college-entrance student" are familiar appellations in almost every high school. The standard fare for college preparatory students is academic subjects like algebra, chemistry, and foreign languages, while vocational subjects, general mathematics, business English, and the like become the subjects most appropriate for those students not so designated. There are unfortunate consequences of these divisions. For one thing, certain segments of the school population have limited exposure to the major disciplines of knowledge. As a result, high-status knowledge is provided for some and not for others, and this may have a restricting effect on one's life chances. For another, the disciplines themselves are demeaned by intimating that the only reason for studying them is to provide access to college.

Although it is unquestionably true that the vast majority of colleges expect a certain pattern of studies for admission, high schools must share the blame for this unfortunate state of affairs. Over the course of roughly a century, many high school reformers have exhibited an only half-concealed tendency to demean the kind of academic knowledge that colleges have come to represent. It is unquestionably the case that colleges from time to time have been dismissive of the kind of experimentation in curriculum matters that some high schools legitimately have undertaken, but the point of view of the colleges is one that needs to be taken seriously. Although academic subjects have acquired something of a new legitimacy in recent years, the secondary-school curriculum is still seen by many reformers as reflecting the yoke of college domination. This essay reviews some of the historical landmarks in this antagonism and suggests some bases for establishing a common ground.

The ladder system in education, now a bureaucratic commonplace, is based on the existence of at least three and more likely four familiar institutions. To be educated in this country, one first enters elementary school, proceeds in carefully graded steps through about 6 years of schooling, then comes to a 3-year junior high school or middle school, next to a high school of usually 4 years, and finally, for a significant number of Americans, enters college. That last stage is in certain respects different and more important than the others. First, education through most of the secondary-school years is typically compulsory, whereas college represents a voluntary commitment, at least insofar as financial resources or, in a few instances, scholarship aid permits. Second, status-attainment studies seem to indicate that while length of schooling through the secondary-school years bears a modest relationship to various measures of success in later life, that relationship begins to approach greater significance when college education is concerned. Finally, when one makes the transition from high school to college, one enters into an educational world that is substantially different in many respects from what one has experienced in the previous 12 years or so. It no longer is simply a higher rung on the educational ladder; it is one that is not governed by a massive system of certification and other state controls for its professional personnel. Hence, its faculty, on the whole, reflect not just different training but different professional commitments as well as a much higher degree of autonomy. At the tertiary level, faculty tend to be committed to the virtues of academic scholarship and the mastery of the disciplines of knowledge. While this commitment is shared by some faculty in elementary and secondary schools, the latter tend to identify more closely with education tied to "real life" and to a more functionally oriented curriculum.

As the twentieth century progressed, an increasing alienation and even antagonism evolved between colleges on one hand and earlier levels of schooling on the other. Even at the beginning of the twenty-first century, an atmosphere of belligerence can be detected here and there in the groves of academe with respect to elementary and secondary teachers and their counterparts in college and university departments of education. One side tends to be seen as excessively utilitarian in outlook and correspondingly less demanding in terms of scholarly attainment, while the other is seen as the upholders of academic rigor and intellectual culture.

It sometimes is forgotten that the familiar educational ladder, as we now know it, is a rather recent development—a product essentially of the twentieth century. The high school did not replace the academy as the predominant form of secondary education until the 1880s. Prior to that and for some years following, admission to college was based to a large extent on individual, sometimes informal, examinations by individual colleges, sometimes without reference to whether the applicant had even attended secondary school. The Carnegie unit as a method of counting credits in high school, and incidentally as a way of calculating admission to college, was not invented until 1906. In the nineteenth century, many students simply showed up at the college of their choice, were examined in certain subjects of study (often particular texts), and then admitted or not admitted on the basis of their performance. In these circumstances, high school teachers at least were partners with their counterparts in the colleges in the common enterprise of getting students into college, and their respective views of what subjects were most important were essentially congruent. The route from partnership to hostility between high schools and colleges may be seen as proceeding in three stages, each characterized by a significant event that more or less symbolizes the growing conflict.

DID THE COMMITTEE OF TEN IMPOSE COLLEGE DOMINATION ON HIGH SCHOOLS?

The National Education Association's Report of the Committee of Ten,[1] long regarded as one of the most significant events in the history of American education, is best known for the four "programmes" of study it recommended, each now commonly characterized, anachronistically, as a "college-entrance" course of study. In fact, it can be argued that the significance of the Committee of Ten's report, especially as it relates to high school–college relations, lies more in the mythology of interpretation that followed its publication than in the actual recommendations espoused by the Committee under its esteemed chairman, Charles W. Eliot, president of Harvard University.

It sometimes is overlooked that the impetus for the National Education Association's appointment of the Committee was the chaos that was developing about college admissions. With each college establishing its own distinctive pattern of admission, sometimes down to the particular text to be studied, high school principals found it almost impossible to create any order out of the high school course of study. A college admissions system that had been established with private tutoring or academy preparation, not high school credits, in mind was simply not suited to the institution of the high school. Much has been made in latter-day interpretations of the impact of the Committee of Ten report that most of the committee members were drawn from colleges, and this has led to the widely accepted notion that the real business of the Committee was to impose college domination on the high school, a task that it is widely credited with accomplishing. Eliot, after all, was the long-standing president of Harvard University, and the other nine members included Henry C. King, a professor at Oberlin College; the president of Vassar College, James M. Taylor; Richard H. Jesse, president of the University of Missouri; the president of Michigan University, James B. Angell; and James H. Baker, president of the University of Colorado. The remaining four members, drawn from the ranks of school administrators, were William Torrey Harris, U.S. Commissioner of Education, but also a long-time superintendent of schools in St. Louis; James Tetlow, principal of the Boston Girls' High and Latin Schools; Oscar D. Robinson, principal of Albany's high school in New York; and James C. Mackenzie, headmaster of the Lawrenceville School in New Jersey, a well-known private secondary school. With the majority of the Committee drawn from the ranks of colleges, it was natural to assume that they brought with them the outlook and biases distinctive to higher education rather than to secondary schools.

In some sense, however, the composition of the Committee was fortuitous. One important task of the Committee was to persuade colleges to accept some uniformity in terms of high school attainment, essentially substituting completion of approved high school programs of study for individual examinations as a basis of admission. Colleges had to be confident that the completion of a given program of studies in high school was a legitimate basis for college admission. In any case, the four "programmes" recommended by the Committee bore a striking resemblance to what high schools were teaching anyway. In fact, to the extent that they departed from standard curricula of the day, it was in the direction of liberalizing the college admissions standards that were then in vogue. In the classical course of study, for example, only 2 years of Greek were required instead of the customary 3. After the report was issued, some of the sharpest criticism directed at Eliot came from the professors of Greek at Harvard, who charged Eliot essentially with selling out. A more important departure from the customary practice in college admissions was the exclusion of Latin from two of the four programs and the substitution of modern foreign languages. In its time, this was a reform of some consequence, since it loosened the grip that the classical languages had long held on college admissions. The main thrust of the committee argument was that high schools should develop the best programs they could for "life" and that colleges should then accept these programs for college admission. It was, therefore, the colleges that were being asked to give up some of their sovereignty. When modern interpreters see a pattern of college domination in the Committee of Ten's recommendations, they are revealing their own latter-day ideas about what constitutes an appropriate curriculum for life, not reflecting the realities of high school–college relations in the 1890s.

It is also important to keep in mind that the Committee of Ten report is an artifact of an era when the ideological gap between the interests of high schools and those of colleges was not nearly as great as it later became. The National Education Association, for example, included among its membership many college professors and college presidents interested in improving American education at all rungs of the educational ladder. Before his appointment to head the Committee, Eliot had been active in the organization and had proposed some far-reaching reforms in elementary and secondary schools. In general, the interests of the high schools and colleges, although obviously not identical, were far more congruent than in later periods. The difference in status and educational outlook between a high school teacher of history and a college history professor, for example, was not nearly as wide as it is today.

The story of an elitist Committee imposing college control over the high school, however, fits very neatly into a mythology that is in fact drawn not from historical reality but from ideological conflict. If one proceeds from the assumption that literature, science, history, algebra, and foreign languages are appropriate only for a select college-entrance population of the high school and not for the mass of high school students, then it becomes difficult to account for their persistence in the high school curriculum. How convenient it is, then, to discover in the Committee of Ten's recommendations the seeds of a successful coup by elitist professors and college presidents, instead of seeking the reasons for their persistence elsewhere. Not the report itself but its place in the mythology of certain school reformers becomes the opening wedge in what was eventually to develop into a gaping chasm between high school and college.

THE EIGHT-YEAR STUDY (1933–1941)

Another singular and much-celebrated event in the development of high school–college relations also had its beginning in the issue of college-entrance requirements. In the 4 decades that intervened between the Committee of Ten and the inception of the Progressive Education Association's Eight-Year Study, a series of differing reform thrusts entered massively upon the American educational scene. By the early 1930s, some of these different ideological thrusts had found their home in the Progressive Education Association (PEA). While these ideological positions maintained their own identities to some extent, the 1930s was also a period when change itself was in the air. As leaders of various reform movements were arguing the case for changes in particular directions, schools were quietly amalgamating pieces of all of them. It was more important for local school administrators to convey to their constituencies that things were up-to-date than to adopt a consistent and coherent program of curriculum reform. Therefore, it was not unusual for individual school districts to adopt changes that in some sense conflicted with one another, tending, for example, to incorporate at one and the same time reforms that might be considered romantically child-centered on one hand and strict standards of performance that reflected mainly cold efficiency on the other.

A source of considerable concern, however, was the apparent recalcitrance of the high school as compared with the elementary school. Given greater flexibility as to structure, the elementary school was in a better position to experiment, particularly with new combinations or recombinations of school subjects, whereas the high school, dominated as it was by rigid bell schedules and departments organized according to particular school subjects, remained more resistant to the impetus for change that dominated the 1930s and earlier. The more convenient villain in the piece, however, was college domination. One prominent leader of the PEA, Wilford M. Aiken, for example, declared in 1931 that "there are no truly progressive secondary schools, in spite of many attempts to create them."[2] The attempts at reform were being thwarted by the demands of colleges that certain courses be offered as part of a college-entrance requirement. By the 1930s, the charge that the Committee of Ten had successfully imposed college domination on American secondary education had become conventional wisdom.

In response to Aiken's call, Harold Rugg of Teachers College proposed that a new committee of the PEA be created, significantly called the Committee on the Relation of School and College (although variations in the name appear in various documents), to address the problem. By 1932, the Carnegie Foundation and the General Education Board had awarded the PEA almost three-quarters of a million dollars for this purpose. A plan was developed whereby colleges would agree temporarily to accept high school graduates from a select group of 30 experimental high schools without reference to their particular pattern of preparation. The students from these experimental high schools would then be matched with students from other high schools who had followed a traditional pattern of college preparation, and their success in college would be plotted. Eventually, some 3,600 students were involved. Heading this monumental undertaking was Ralph Tyler, who was brought from the Bureau of Educational Research at Ohio State University to be its research director. The intent of the experiment was to demonstrate that the traditional pattern of college preparation offered high school graduates no particular advantage insofar as college success was concerned. Once that was shown, the leaders of the PEA believed, the shackles of college domination perpetrated by the Committee of Ten would be broken, and high schools as well as elementary schools would be free to depart from the traditional mold as to curriculum.

The 30 "unshackled" high schools, as they came to be called, were free to change their programs of study in virtually any direction. In fact, there was enormous variation in the way these schools exercised their newfound freedom. At the North Country Day School of Winnetka, Illinois, it was reported that the Latin program had eliminated "such stupid material as the Cataline Orations" and had replaced them with 20 to 25 of Cicero's letters as well as about the same number from Pliny.[3] New Trier Township High School reported that it revised its English curriculum to include an 8-week study of drama, working back chronologically from the modern play through Shakespeare to the ancient Greek dramatists.[4] Wisconsin High School, on the other hand, a campus school, introduced a radical curriculum organized around "areas of living," with the four constants being community living, health, vocations, and leisure time, the constants accounting for approximately two-thirds of the school day.[5] In Tulsa, Oklahoma, a select group of high school students were required to enroll in a 2-hour-a-week "Social Relations" program.[6] Obviously, the unshackled high schools were using the freedom to innovate in quite different ways. The experimental variable in the whole massive undertaking that was the Eight-Year Study, if one can be identified at all, was change itself. The graduates of the 30 unshackled schools had all come from high schools that had changed in some way, but no well-defined direction to the change is actually identifiable.

The results, once they began to trickle in during the 1939–40 academic year, came as something of an anticlimax. When such traditional criteria of success as grade-point average were used, the graduates of the unshackled schools neither "set the colleges on fire"[7] nor compared unfavorably with their counterparts from the control group drawn from traditional high schools. The PEA derived some consolation from the fact that the experimental group came out "*a little ahead.*"[8] Actually, even that ambiguous result should have been a victory for those who sought to break the yoke of college domination, since, at a minimum, it indicated that the standard pattern of college preparation offered no particular advantage in terms of college success. No notable changes in the national pattern of college-entrance requirements, however, emerged from the Eight-Year Study.

Various reasons have been offered for the negligible impact of this massive experiment on high school–college relations. Most prominently mentioned is the fact that the five-volume report was published just after America's entry into World War II, when, it is argued, the minds of Americans were not on the issue of college preparation. In retrospect, however, it appears naive to assume that the interests of public school people on one hand and academicians in colleges and universities on the other would give way in the face of results from a single experiment, however ambitious and far-reaching. Even beyond that, for a half century before the results of the Eight-Year Study were published, American education had been a battleground for various educational doctrines. Although the three major reform thrusts, developmentalism, social efficiency, and social meliorism, differed dramatically from one another, virtually their only common thread was their mutual antagonism to the kind of traditional humanist curriculum that had been espoused by Eliot and the Committee of Ten. That position had become practically expunged from the thinking of school reformers, even though the traditional subjects of study that constituted the humanist curriculum continued to appear prominently in elementary- and secondary-school programs of study. In a sense, the last stronghold of the liberal arts ideal, in terms of advocacy at least, resided in the colleges and universities. It was the likes of Robert Maynard Hutchins, Mortimer Adler, and Jacques Maritain, speaking from their perches in the major universities of the country, who defended the virtues of the organized disciplines of knowledge, while the opposition came from those who claimed to speak for elementary and secondary schools. Thus the ideological rift that had been barely visible in the days of the Committee of Ten report was now considerably widened. It was no longer the colleges and the high schools working together on common problems from a reasonably coherent point of view, but the high schools *against* the colleges. The colleges had, by and large, become the upholders of one tradition, and the high schools of some others. They were viewing the educational process through quite different lenses, and the Eight-Year Study, whatever the outcome, was not going to change that.

THE BATTLE OVER LIFE ADJUSTMENT EDUCATION (1945–1958)

The most dramatic and, in the long run, the most searing confrontation between high school doctrine on one hand and college doctrine on the other had its inception at a White House conference held on May 31 and June 1, 1945 under the general rubric, Vocational Education in the Years Ahead. Eventually, the participants turned to Charles A. Prosser, the longtime director of the Dunwoody Institute in Minneapolis and a veteran proponent in the battle to pass the Smith–Hughes Act in 1918, to summarize the proceedings. Rising to the challenge, Prosser proposed a resolution declaring that 20% of high school youth were being well served by the college-entrance programs and another 20% by the vocational programs, but that 60% of high school students were not receiving the life adjustment training they needed. The Conference Committee adopted that resolution unanimously, and the life adjustment movement was born.

Although throughout its existence, life adjustment education faced a problem of definition, its basic thrust was anti-academic in the sense that many of the programs that bore its name sought to replace the traditional subjects of study, those that formed the backbone of the Committee of Ten recommendations, with subjects built around what generally were called areas of living (like the ones that Wisconsin High School introduced during the Eight-Year Study). For example, one stalwart of the life adjustment movement declared, "Reduced to its simplest terms, [life adjustment education] stands for *an adequate program of secondary education for fairly complete preparation for all the areas of living in which life adjustment must be made, particularly home living, vocational life, civic life, leisure life, and physical and mental health.*"[9] What had been the subject of some experimentation during the period of the Eight-Year Study was now proposed for all high schools. Even the rather dubious percentage figures that Prosser included in his resolution were gradually forgotten in favor life adjustment education for all.

Life adjustment education received the enthusiastic support of a large segment of the professional education community. The National Association of Secondary-School Principals, for example, sponsored several "discussion groups" in an effort to implement the program, and their *Bulletin* carried a steady stream of articles extolling its virtues. The Superintendent of Public Instruction of the State of Illinois saw life adjustment education as redressing an unwholesome emphasis on academics with a healthy dose of "real-life problems." The test of a good school, he felt, could be enunciated as follows: "If the products of our schools turn out to be healthy and patriotic citizens who are good husbands, good wives, good fathers, good mothers, good neighbors, good workers, good employers, wise spenders of income, wholesome users of leisure time and so forth, we know that our schools are good."[10] Commissioner of Education John W. Studebaker was quoted by *Newsweek* as prophesying that, under the new regime of life adjustment education, "old standbys like Milton's 'Il Pensoroso' and George Eliot's 'Silas Marner' would probably disappear from the schools."[11]

Life adjustment education turned out to be the prod that stirred the academic world into action. Clearly, the major tenets of life adjustment education, being so vigorously promoted by the leadership in elementary and secondary schools, ran contrary to the instincts and convictions of the faculties of colleges and universities. After half a century of neglect, the academic community began to take a deep interest in what was going on in elementary and secondary schools, and many of their pronouncements reflected a passion and an animosity rarely heard in academic discourse. Harry J. Fuller, a college professor and early critic not only of the state of education but of professors of education, cited some statements by what he described as "the foe" and declared them to be "rubbish . . . consistent and colossal rubbish."[12] Indeed, leaders in elementary and secondary education on one side and academicians interested in schooling at the elementary and secondary levels on the other had become "foes." The relatively minor antagonisms that derived from questions of articulation as one moved from one rung of the educational ladder to the next had become a major ideological rift. High school and college were no longer simply different institutions; they were populated with faculties holding quite different views as to what American education should be like.

Probably the most trenchant of the academic critics was Arthur E. Bestor, Jr., a professor of history at the University of Illinois. His basic argument was that elementary and secondary education had been diverted from its central function, the development of the intellect. In an effort to make high schools directly functional for future living, educational leaders had crossed the line into anti-intellectualism. Bestor, for example, ridiculed the vague inclusiveness of the ten Imperative Needs of Youth, a major life adjustment document that defined the role of high schools in terms of meeting "the common and specific needs of youth." It is not, he argued, the role of the high schools to meet student needs in some general sense while neglecting intellectual training. He also saw the life adjustment movement as blatantly antidemocratic. Bestor interpreted the 60% figure in the original Prosser resolution as meaning that most people "are incapable of being benefitted by intellectual training," arguing that such a division in the high school population "enthrones once again the ancient doctrine that the majority of people are destined from birth to be hewers of wood and drawers of water to a select few who, by right of superior fitness are to occupy the privileged places in society,"[13] a position reminiscent of Eliot's defense of the Committee of Ten's recommendations. Eliot had once argued that schools had no right to decide what roles their students eventually should play in society and, therefore, determining the curriculum on the basis of probable destination of students should have no place in school policy.[14]

The academicians won the battle over life adjustment education and have been consolidating their position ever since. When Sputnik was launched in October 1957, it put the rift between school and college leaders squarely in the context of the cold war, and media coverage clearly favored the critics like Bestor. By the 1980s, criticism of American elementary and secondary schools had become a popular pastime, with a major share of the blame for the weakness of American education being accorded to college and university departments of education. After about 100 years of growing antagonism in school and college relations, the anti-intellectual tag had stuck.

OUTLOOK IN HIGH SCHOOL–COLLEGE RELATIONS

The intense controversy that erupted between high school and college spokespersons over the merits of life adjustment education represented, in one sense, the culmination of decades of progressively diverging conceptions as to what education is all about. Part of the problem in interpreting the relationship between high school and college over the past century lies in an incomplete understanding of the major ideological positions that vied for control of the American curriculum. What emerged in the life adjustment era, for example, was not a monolithic position representing the so-called progressive forces in American education. Quite the reverse, it represented in the main only one line of reform, social efficiency, a doctrine that held up social stability and, of course, supreme efficiency as the criteria of excellence for American schools. With efficiency as the ultimate standard, it was not surprising that literature, history, and higher mathematics as well as other academic subjects should have such low status. These subjects, after all, have little direct utility. They do not function in any obvious way in our daily lives. Academicians did well to question some of social efficiency's basic assumptions, but so did thoughtful school reformers such as Boyd Bode.[15] And it must be admitted that the charge of anti-intellectualism on the part of the academic critics had considerable validity when applied to certain, but by no means all, of the proposed reforms.

What is unfortunate, however, is that disparate efforts to reconstruct the American elementary and secondary curriculum over the course of the twentieth century have been regarded as largely all of one piece. There are, in other words, reforms, and then there are reforms. Bestor, interestingly enough, unlike some of the other critics, was enough of a scholar to recognize that expressions of the policy of life adjustment education had no relevance to the work of John Dewey.[16] They were in fact antagonistic to one another. And yet those of us who should know better continue to lump together several distinctive, even conflicting, strands of American educational reform into a potpourri we call progressive education. *Reform* is one of those words that carries with it uniformly positive connotations, but there were some "reforms" that were unquestionably anti-progressive and, as Bestor claimed, even anti-intellectual. Given the understandable commitment of colleges and universities to intellectual development, it is these perceived or actual anti-intellectual tendencies embedded in certain proposed curriculum reforms of the twentieth century that have been the most persistent source of high school–college antagonism. From the melange of reforms that have been proposed, we need to disentangle those, like Dewey's, that were directed at strengthening the intellect, not only of the college-going population but of all future citizens, from those that were directed primarily at converting schools into an engine for the sorting and classifying of future citizens according to probable destination, such as the widely accepted secondary-school classifications of college entrance and noncollege entrance. Once we are able to identify and reflect upon the ingredients that went into that potpourri, sorting out the crassly utilitarian from the genuinely educative, we will be in a much better position to resolve the more-than-a-century-old split between schools and colleges.

Certainly, one common ground between the high school and the college is the mutual interest in the development of sound and responsible thinking, not for the few, but for all. At the secondary-school level, the value of the study of subjects like chemistry, mathematics, and foreign languages has to be seen not merely as a ticket for college (as the term "college-entrance subject" so clearly implies), but as vital ingredients of our culture, appropriate not for a select segment of the school population but for the vast majority. From the perspective of the colleges, the academic disciplines of knowledge have to be seen not simply as rarefied abstractions divorced from common experience but as emerging from widely shared human purposes, impulses, and aspirations. The commitment to excellence on the part of colleges needs to be augmented by a sense that the connections between academic knowledge and those human purposes have to be made more explicitly visible.

CHAPTER 5

Harold Rugg and the Reconstruction of the Social Studies Curriculum: The Treatment of the "Great War" in His Textbook Series

CO-AUTHORED WITH GREG WEGNER

Pessimism about school reform has reached the point where it is easy to overlook some actual accomplishments. There are some notable instances of success, and they may provide some clues as to why certain reforms fizzle while others make their way triumphantly into school practice. During the period of the Great Depression, a reform movement that became known as social reconstructionism began to gain considerable recognition in education circles. As America's economic picture became increasingly bleak, social reconstructionists sought to ameliorate conditions through a curriculum that would directly address such problems as poverty, inequality, and unemployment. In a bold and stirring address before the Progressive Education Association in 1932, George S. Counts actually dared schools to build a new social order.[1] Much of social reconstructionism, however, was confined to heated debates among leaders in education, with little of that ideology actually making its way into school practice. An exception was the astounding success of a series of social studies textbooks that were written by Harold O. Rugg, Counts's colleague at Teachers College, Columbia University. Through those textbooks, thousands of young Americans were introduced to the social critiques and interpretations that were part and parcel of social reconstructionism.

One concrete example was Rugg's treatment of World War I. Rather than concentrating on the standard causes of the Great War, such as the assassination of Archduke Ferdinand, Rugg sought to emphasize such controversial topics as the role of propaganda, militarism, and secret diplomacy in touching off the conflagration. This essay examines the particular ways Rugg departed from the typical textbook treatment of war as he sought to transmit the ideas of those he called "frontier thinkers" to a new generation of readers. Although his ideas were quite radical for their time, his manner of introducing them—through textbooks—followed a time-honored tradition that did not violate what David Tyack and Larry Cuban have called aptly "the grammar of schooling."[2] Likewise, although Rugg sought a reconstruction of the way social studies was taught, he did not challenge the school subject as the basic building block of the curriculum as did other reformers. Rugg's success is probably attributable to the fact that the reforms he introduced, radical as they were in political terms, were consistent with basic structures of schooling.

If one were to judge the changes in the American curriculum from the turn of the twentieth century to the present by the extent to which certain subjects actually replaced others or by the addition of major new subjects to the curriculum, one would likely find only moderate alterations. From a list of subjects alone, one might note, for example, that what was once a heavy emphasis on Latin and a lesser emphasis on Greek, was replaced by the study of modern foreign languages. Perhaps the single most dramatic curriculum change in the course of the twentieth century was the massive entry of vocational education in its various manifestations into the school curriculum, accompanied by such satellite additions as business English and commercial arithmetic. It would be misleading, however, to judge the extent of the transformation in the American curriculum by such readily visible changes alone. Perhaps the most significant, albeit subtle, changes occurred *within* the context of some of the individual subject areas. English, for example, in 1900 was not the same subject that is being taught under the same name at the beginning of the twenty-first century.

RECONSTRUCTING THE SOCIAL STUDIES

One of the most significant of these internal transformations involves not simply a name change (from history and other individual disciplines to social studies) but a massive reconceptualization of a subject area. The reconstruction of the social studies took place essentially in two stages. One involved the efforts of Thomas Jesse Jones of Hampton Institute (among others) during the first 2 decades of the twentieth century to redirect the social studies along practical lines in keeping with the dominant curriculum doctrine of social efficiency. It was that reform that constituted the first serious challenge to the traditional academic emphasis in the teaching of the social studies and made civic virtue and an efficiently functioning citizenry the dominant ideal. The second line of reform, proceeding in a very different direction, was spearheaded by the work of Harold Rugg, beginning in the 1920s and extending into the early 1940s, to change both the form and the ideological direction of the social studies. His great ambition was to create a fused social studies out of the several individual disciplines that traditionally had been present in the curriculum in an earlier era, and at the same time to inject into that study a vision of a new America and indeed a new world. That effort reached its peak in the 1930s with the growing popularity of his textbook series, *Man and His Changing Society*.

Rugg's career virtually represents in miniature the panorama of educational ideologies that characterized twentieth-century curriculum reform in America: scientific curriculum making, child-centered education, and, most notably, social reconstructionism. Rugg's first major change in direction occurred when he abandoned his original studies in civil engineering to undertake a doctorate in education at the University of Illinois, studying with William Chandler Bagley. After being awarded the degree in 1915, he accepted an appointment in the faculty of education at the University of Chicago, which, under the leadership of Charles Hubbard Judd, aspired to become the citadel of the scientific study of education. Six years later, as an associate professor at Teachers College, Columbia University, and an educational psychologist for its Lincoln School, he undertook his massive campaign to reconstruct the social studies.

Although Rugg had long been interested in the social studies as a school subject, his particular ideas on how it should be reconstructed were most likely influenced by his new associations in New York. Rugg himself notes that his move to Teachers College represented "a sharp turning point in my life marking the beginning of a new period—many years of unlearning and an exciting search for understanding."[3] Something of this transformation in Rugg's thinking had been foreshadowed 2 years earlier by his meeting with Arthur Upham Pope, a remarkable intellectual who had given up a career as a professor of philosophy to devote himself to the study of Persian art, ultimately becoming one of the world's foremost scholars on that subject. It was Rugg's meeting with Pope in 1918 (while working on an army project) and their later friendship that first led Rugg to take stock of the "one long orgy of tabulation"[4] that had been so central to his earlier work. He was later to reflect on "how seldom most of us fact finders really found the 'right' facts."[5] His removal to Teachers College and his associations with New York intellectuals and artists helped nourish the seed that Pope had planted. In Rugg's words, he "left [Charles Hubbard] Judd's ordered team of 'scientists' and joined [Otis W.] Caldwell's company of creative individualists."[6]

Like Pope, many of these intellectuals with whom Rugg now associated combined left-wing social criticism with avant-garde artistic interests. The new humanism of Waldo Frank, the unflinching pacifism of Randolph Bourne, and the reinterpretations of America's literary traditions as advanced by Van Wyck Brooks seemed to mesh in Rugg's mind with artistic trends that were being advanced at that time by such innovators in the arts as Georgia O'Keefe, Isidora Duncan, and Alfred Stieglitz. The influence of Rugg's friendships with these New York intellectuals fortified his decision to re-evaluate his earlier commitment to a "science" of education in the direction of a new appreciation of creative artistry combined with social criticism. Were it not for the stimulating associations that Rugg found in his new environment, his work, and, in particular, his attempt to create a new social studies surely would have taken a decidedly different turn.

Early in the 1920s, Rugg seems to have begun to consider a reconstruction of the form of the social studies curriculum as well as its content. In particular, he conceived of the idea that a social studies course could be developed around "the great principles or generalizations in history, economics, industry, geography, etc."[7] These principles, of course, were consistent with the ideas that he found in the New York intellectual environment. Additionally, in Rugg's mind, the existence of these separate subjects as representative of the social studies was a prime example of unwarranted fragmentation in the curriculum. As against such rigid compartmentalization in the organization of the curriculum, Rugg held out the ideal of a unified social studies that would be constructed around the major generalizations as enunciated by leaders in various branches of the social studies: "Rather than have teachers attempt the almost impossible task of correlating history, geography, civics, economics and sociology (taught as separate subjects), we postulate that more effective outcomes will be secured by weaving together lesson by lesson the facts, movements, conditions, that depend upon one another and that can be fully comprehended only when they are woven together."[8] Rugg thus was searching for a way of conceptualizing the social studies that would integrate them rather than have them appear in the school curriculum as a disjointed series of separate entities.

One early manifestation of the direction he was to take was reflected in his response to an address delivered by Henry Johnson to the Teachers College faculty. Johnson spoke on behalf of the American Historical Association and the Joint Committee on History and Education for Citizenship, one of several bodies convened by the American Historical Society to explore improvement in the history curriculum. Those committees had been working intermittently on the history curriculum ever since the Committee of Seven delivered its recommendations in 1899.[9] The brunt of Rugg's criticism of the Joint Committee's recommendations was that the defense of the traditional subject-matter triad of history, civics, and geography by the American Historical Association evaded any real reform in the social studies. Reflecting his early faith in a science of curriculum making, he chided the Joint Committee for making proposals "without controlled and measured experimentation."[10] But along with Rugg's call for the use of the scientific method in the creation of the social studies curriculum, there was a strongly voiced expression of need for more activity on the part of children, along with less compartmentalization in the curriculum. Significantly, Rugg also cited "social worth" as the basis from which curriculum makers could develop materials for the classroom, in light of the vital problems of contemporary life. Rugg's conception of what was socially worthy put him directly at odds with other major curriculum leaders of the period, such as Franklin Bobbitt, W. W. Charters, and David Snedden.

Some of those ideas on the reconstruction of the social studies curriculum may have been fermenting in Rugg's mind since 1916 when he and Bagley undertook an examination of 23 American history textbooks used in junior high schools. Not surprisingly, Bagley and Rugg discovered that textbook writers placed a heavy emphasis on political and military affairs. In combination with the growing standardization of elementary textbooks, they felt that the social studies were presenting a narrow focus on political developments at the expense of larger social and economic issues in world affairs. Their study concluded with a statement on the implications of a nationalistic view of history for the social studies curriculum:

> The fact is that the obvious influence of the elementary textbook in history today is distinctly toward the promotion of nationalism through giving to all the pupils who reach the seventh and eighth years of school life a common stock of information regarding national development. The important question at the present juncture would seem to center on the desirability or undesirability of making the development of nationalism the primary function of seventh and eighth grade history. This is an issue that is fraught with consequences far too fundamental to be settled by any single group of individuals.[11]

It was this kind of deficiency that Rugg later sought to correct in his own Junior High School Course, which was to gain widespread acceptance in the 1930s.

In 1921–22, Rugg embarked on an ambitious effort to replace the tame and frankly nationalistic social studies textbooks of the day with a series that would embody the basic principles of social worth as to content and the integration of previously separated fields in terms of form. The actual task of extracting the needed generalizations from the works of the leading political and social progressives of the day fell to his doctoral student, Neal Billings. From a list of works that were written by what Rugg called "frontier thinkers," Billings identified no fewer than 888 generalizations from such diverse disciplines as sociology, economics, political science, and geography. History, as a discipline, was not mentioned by name, although the works of Charles Beard as well as other historians appeared on the final list.[12]

One of Rugg's principal points of attack on the traditional history curriculum centered on the memorization of specific facts. It was not Rugg's intention to ignore historical facts. On the contrary, the Rugg social studies curriculum sought to maintain a strong continuity with other programs in terms of building a mastery of concepts, facts, and meanings. What placed Rugg's series apart from the other curricula of the day was the special emphasis given to the relationships among facts, a process that Rugg felt was definitively expressed by what he liked to call generalizing, "that process of recognizing in a series of situations, events, objects, etc. one or more characters, traits or items that are alike, common to all."[13] If repetition was to play any role in social studies education, as Rugg told the American Historical Association in 1921, it was to be in making the interconnections between the great economic, social, and political laws, movements, and causal relations. Thinking was something a student needed to practice, and the generalizations were presented as the "glue" in teaching higher thought processes.

The treatment of the Great War in his textbook series provides one dramatic illustration of Rugg's attempt, on one hand, to rescue the teaching of the social studies from the dry memorization of facts and, on the other, to infuse socially progressive ideas into the curriculum. The starting point for that task was the key generalizations on the subject that Billings had culled from the works of the frontier thinkers. In this regard, Rugg's approach to curriculum design marked another sharp departure from what had become conventional wisdom among the scientific curriculum makers, such as Bobbitt and Charters. They sought to reform the traditional curriculum through the technique they most commonly called activity analysis, an approach borrowed directly from Frederick Winslow Taylor and the widely admired scientific management movement. The basis of activity analysis as a way of constructing a curriculum was first to create a catalog of actual human activity grouped under functional categories such as citizenship activities or leisure activities. The minute behaviors, presumably collected through scientific observation, would then become the objectives of the curriculum. In this way, the scientific curriculum makers argued, the teaching of the various subjects could be rescued from the dry and inert teaching that characterized the typical academic curriculum. A curriculum based on actual observed behavior presumably could be made directly functional in terms of the lives of students. Not incidentally, it also would create a more smoothly functioning society.

Rugg recognized, however, that basing the curriculum on the actual activities that people were already engaging in would most likely lead in the direction of a social status quo. He reacted against the idea that the curriculum should be concerned primarily with preparing youth to perform efficiently in predetermined adult roles. Instead, he sought to equip the next generation with the cutting edge of ideas and principles, ideas that Billings had extracted from the principal works of major scholars. In this way, rather than formulating a curriculum tied to the world as it was, Rugg sought to equip the youth of the nation with the concepts and generalizations that could transform existing social conditions.

RUGG'S TREATMENT OF WORLD WAR I

Inevitably, Rugg's left-wing political commitments found their way into the social studies textbook series *Man and His Changing Society*. To some extent, this was dictated by the initial choice of frontier thinkers and to some extent by the way in which Rugg chose to integrate the generalizations into the overall treatment of the various topics he included in his textbook series. In few other areas was Rugg's protest against existing social conditions greater than in relationship to militarism and war. In particular, Rugg felt compelled to challenge students' thinking on the legacy of World War I and to call attention to the prospects for human survival through international cooperation.[15]

In order to illustrate the prevalence of certain concepts in the 888 generalizations, Billings calculated a combined "cause" and "result" score for each concept appearing more than once among the mass of generalizations. The concepts,

Billings claimed, "must build up" in order to make effective use of generalizations in the thinking process. The building to which Billings referred involved a series of calculations in which each concept, either as a cause or effect factor in the historical process, was assessed one point for each time it either appeared in the generalizations or was mentioned more than once in books written by the frontier thinkers.[16] Given this system of calculation, out of a total of 505 concepts, war ranked twenty-first, military conquest, fifty-seventh, and militarism, seventy-second. Interestingly, war was viewed more often as a cause than as a result in the generalizations, whereas the reverse was true for military conquest. Militarism, understandably, was most likely to appear in the Billings scheme as a cause for war (see generalization 589 in Billings, p. 175).

Billings's own categories of war and international relations, imperialism, diplomacy, boundaries, and international trade can be used to group ideas taken from the frontier thinkers:

War and International Relations

592. Other things being equal, that society will stand the best chance of survival which has the largest population. [Charles A. Ellwood, *Sociology and Modern Social Problems*, p. 168]

593. Political coordination and war are alternative in determining the relations which chief population groups must sustain to each other in order mutually to satisfy their wants by access to resources that only one or the other can supply. [Isaiah Bowman, *The New World: Problems in Political Geography*, p. 59]

594. Climate, no doubt, is the key to many of the invasions and conquests which have bent the current of history again and again. [Edward A. Ross, *Principles of Sociology*, p. 68]

595. The causes of war are many. Some underlying factors leading to war are:

Psychological factors of human nature—hatred, rivalries, ambitions and the like [Graham Wallas, *Human Nature in Politics*, p. 16; Ellsworth Huntington, *Principles of Human Geography*, p. 98; Richard H. Tawney, *The Acquisitive Society*, p. 42; Ellen Semple, *Influences of Geographic Environment*, p. 552; Bowman, pp. 1, 11, 305]
Ignorance of past history [Harold Stearns, *Civilization in the United States*, p. 307]
Struggle for food supply [Ellwood, p. 48; Semple, p. 586]
Increase in population [Ellwood, p. 48; Bowman, p. 502]
Tariff tinkering [Richard T. Ely, *Outlines of Economics*, p. 360]
Imposition or attempted imposition of ideas and power of one people on another. [Bowman, p. 565]

596. A treaty which is not signed by the representatives of the people whom the treaty affects does not of itself settle disorder or kill political ambitions. [Bowman, p. 61]

597. In general, the more nearly matched are two combatants, the more prolonged and exhausting their conflict is likely to be. [Ross, p. 178]

598. The consciousness of a common purpose in mankind, or even the acknowledgement that such a common purpose is possible, would alter the face of world politics at once. [Wallas, p. 306]

Imperialism

587. Nations impelled with a desire to secure markets gradually absorb weak countries. [Bowman, p. 564]

588. If leaders can get their people to believe that they are hemmed in by enemies and that openings everywhere invite attack, and to become sufficiently "jumpy" about it, they can impose heavy taxes for large armies that are not meant for the defense of the country, but for the aggrandizement and the satisfaction of greed. [Bowman, p. 348]

589. Militarism strangles liberal political development and strengthens imperialistic tendencies. [Ross, p. 684]

Diplomacy

583. Secrecy in the conduct of diplomacy is vital in a world where each nation is suspicious of its neighbors and obliged by its fears to try to discover their plans while concealing its own. [James Bryce, *Modern Democracies*, Vol. I, p. 54]

Boundaries

449. War is often followed by a change in boundaries. [Semple, p. 183]

International Trade

149. Famines, wars and scientific discoveries will make some trades expand and others dwindle. [Beatrice Webb and Sidney Webb, *Industrial Democracy*, p. 745]

177. War often curtails the capacity to export goods and increases the demand for imports. [Ely, p. 353][17]

These generalizations constituted a clear departure from the predominant political emphasis on human conflict that has characterized much history textbook writing to this day. To the extent that Rugg was able to incorporate the generalizations in his textbook series, the multifaceted interpretations of historical process inherent in the generalizations on war conveyed to young readers that the importance of World War I in human history extended far beyond the assassination at Sarajevo and the political settlement at Versailles, into the realms of international trade, imperialism, diplomatic relations, and propaganda (588).

Since Rugg was especially concerned with developing problems from contemporary history, it is not surprising that World War I, rather than earlier wars, was the most frequently used time frame for communicating the war generalizations. Of the 19 generalizations concerning war, 17 were developed within the context of the Great War. Of the two remaining generalizations, Ellwood's statement (592) relating societal survival to population size apparently was not included in any part of the Rugg series; Ross's comment (594) on the influence of climate on invasion and conquest was integrated by Rugg in his brief account of Napoleon's defeat in Russia during the winter of 1812–13, but was not included in any section on World War I.[18]

Rugg's treatment of the Great War gave scant attention to portraying the details of battle strategy or even the names of the more well-known clashes. On the other hand, he did take considerable pains to list the financial and human costs of the war. Of all the texts, Rugg devoted the most space to World War I in Volume Two, *Changing Civilizations in the Modern World*. It was in this text that we find the greatest contrast in coverage between the military and cause-and-effect dimensions of "the war to end all wars." In a 26-page chapter entitled "The Interdependence of Europe in 1914," Rugg discussed the major causes leading to World War I. In the next chapter, "How the World War Changed Europe," eight pages were devoted to the military phase of the war, followed by a 39-page study of the costs of the war and the European recovery. Furthermore, Volume Two developed a higher number of generalizations pertaining to World War I than any other text in the junior high curriculum.

The cause-and-effect dimensions of Rugg's interpretation of World War I, as evidenced in the generalizations, were incorporated to various degrees in three other texts. Invariably, some of these generalizations were expressed in connection with other historical conflicts as well.[19]

In terms of coverage alone, the Rugg texts placed special emphasis on three interrelated causes of World War I. One (595), largely psychological, focused on "hatred, rivalries, ambitions and the like"; the second (583) was predominantly political and involved secret alliances; and the third (587) grew out of economic pressures to secure markets. Given the complexity and difficulty of Billings's task of imposing some kind of order on the multitude of generalizations, it should not be surprising that his classification scheme appears naive here and there in treating certain factors as separate from the causes of the war, for example, the competition to secure world markets and secret diplomacy. Nevertheless, Billings's work in extracting the generalizations from the work of leading social scientists and historians constituted the basis of Rugg's effort to develop an integration of the social studies curriculum.

The meteoric rise to power by the fascist states in Europe and Asia prompted Rugg to reassess his treatment of the boundary provisions and war reparations included in the Treaty of Versailles (see generalization 449). Rugg apparently felt that the Treaty of Versailles was worth only two paragraphs in Volume Two, the first book in the series to introduce students to international relations. When the first edition of Volume Six was published 2 years later, in 1932, Rugg expanded his treatment of the treaty provisions to five pages. Some 4 years after Hitler's *Machtergreifung*, Rugg published his second edition of Volume Six, but this time he interjected a prologue to Versailles. One notes a tone of urgency in his writing: "There seems to be no doubt that the great powers, backed by the largest peace-time armaments in the history of the world, are now lining up for a world struggle. In the midst of this tension, which seems to herald a Second World War . . . democratic countries are asking: What will happen to our way-of-life? Can democracy survive?"[20]

The survival of democracy, in Rugg's mind, was directly related to the existence of an informed citizenry in both war and peace. The reality that political systems were prone to using false propaganda in order to garner support for the furtherance of war aims was an especially critical issue for Rugg. Generalization 588, which indicated that governments can manipulate their populations to support war, represented a major theme in the Rugg social studies curriculum. In his fourth volume, *A History of American Government and Culture*, Rugg brought to his readers one of the most direct attacks on the conduct of the U.S. government in the days leading up to the American entry into the war:

> The American people, accustomed to peace, were educated to support war. Thus, a people who had struggled for nearly 300 years for democracy, thus voluntarily gave up much of their liberty and many of their rights. How could such an attitude come about in a democratic country in which the rights and liberty of the individual were such sacred things? It came about because the government conducted a great campaign of education to convince the people that our country confronted a great crisis and that *while war continued* the government must be given complete power. So with the understanding that it should be only *while the war continued* the people submitted and gave the government dictatorial powers over their very lives.[21]

There is in much of Rugg's textbook writing a kind of Jeffersonian distrust for government, especially those governments that sought an increase in war powers at the expense of domestic policy or improved foreign relations.[22] His social criticism also extended to the political institutions that encouraged the headlong drive toward colonization and market security without giving consideration to the implications for international economic competition and impending war.[23] From

[handwritten marginal note: critical literary — text positions readers]

Rugg's standpoint, in textbooks wars could not be dismissed merely as a result of only one set of circumstances. A complicated interplay of social, political, and economic forces were at work. Billings and Rugg thought that by integrating the social studies generalizations into the text series, they would help students understand the nature of this complexity.[24]

However, the 17 generalizations related to war included in the six volumes of the junior high school series do not by themselves convey a definitive notion of Rugg's outlook on the long-term processes underlying historical change. Although not an avowed Marxist or socialist, Rugg also integrated the concepts of class struggle and property ownership into *Man and His Changing Society*.[25] His treatment of the Industrial Revolution, for example, was based on this kind of interpretation. Indeed, the interrelatedness of class and property ownership remained very much a part of Rugg's conception of war and international relations even though the connection was not explicitly made in the 17 generalizations. What caused World War I, in Rugg's eyes, was not an isolated constellation of political forces. The basic causes of the "war to end all wars" had historical antecedents in much earlier generations, all of whom were tied to the struggle over property rights and social class.[26]

The sixth volume of the series, for example, included a collection of six drawings described as showing "the age-long struggle for property." The reality of conflict over ownership was portrayed by a pack of wolves competing for the carcass of a rabbit, followed by a confrontation between two cavemen over a woman, the attack by ancient Persian armies, the Battle of the Spanish Armada, the overthrow of the British Crown, and American Indians attacking a Conestoga wagon. In a related reading, Rugg summed up his view of historical process for readers, with history defined as "the story of men settling the age-old question: How should property be owned?"

Bagley and Rugg had asserted in their textbook study that the common person usually was omitted from the pages of a majority of history texts because of an undue emphasis on events and what they called "Hall of Fame" personalities.[27] Rugg's series sought to redress that imbalance. In *Changing Civilizations in the Modern World*, Rugg introduced a section on conditions in Europe on the eve of war in 1914 in which he stressed the essential unity of human interests. Most of the population from the belligerent countries, he wrote, did not want war and cared little for the schemes of the major power brokers in expanding foreign markets or hiking arms budgets. Although this interpretation might be regarded by some historians[28] as too simplistic, one cannot deny that Rugg challenged the social studies student to consider the impact of war beyond the treaty obligations and the state of contending armies. Never to be forgotten, if the research group at Lincoln School had anything to say about it, were the countless masses of humanity who "were not especially concerned with the building of the British Empire, nor particularly excited about France's desire to regain Alsace–Lorraine, nor especially upset about Germany's growing control of trade. Most of the people," according to Rugg, "were interested in steady jobs, in good wages, in vacations and in good homes."[29]

With the memory of the Great War still fresh in his mind, Rugg challenged his young readers with the highly controversial historical problem of war guilt. After presenting statistics on the increase in expenditures for arms production in Russia, France, Great Britain, and Germany from 1905 to 1914, Rugg stressed that the vast outlays in weaponry were made possible by the imposition of a staggering tax program "upon the peasants and artisans," with the blessings of all four governments. Furthermore, the biggest enemy of international cooperation and economic interdependence—secret diplomacy—was practiced by the Great Powers and thus gave more credence to the notion that the responsibility for World War I was not rightfully placed in the German camp alone, as the war guilt clause in the Treaty of Versailles suggested.[30]

In many ways, the Rugg textbook project build on the legacy of mass destruction that was World War I in order to warn about the likelihood of another, even more devastating conflict. Rugg was especially inventive in integrating controversial cartoons into his texts in order to make his points clear. In the 1932 edition of *Changing Governments and Changing Cultures*, one cartoon illustrated public frustration with war as a perceived solution to the international chaos unleashed by unchecked nationalism. In the same volume, another cartoon suggested that the world of 1930 was largely out of touch with the lessons of the Great War. When Rugg published his second edition of Volume Six, the consequences of an unbridled arms race had been brought to the fore by the increasing power of fascist states. One cartoon portrayed the end of civilization with a boat sinking under the ominous weight of armaments and carrying with it to the depths the dove of peace.[31]

In no other segment of the Rugg Junior High School Course were students challenged to think about their own attitudes toward the legacy of the Great War more than in the workbooks accompanying the six volumes of text. The workbook for *Changing Civilizations* was especially noteworthy in this regard. In the very first problem, students were asked whether each of 20 items listed elicited an agreeable or disagreeable impression:

How Do You Feel About These Things?

1. "America First"
2. League of Nations
3. Germans
4. Army
5. Jews
6. Russians
7. Military preparedness
8. Disarmament
9. Foreigners

10. Free speech
11. American Legion
12. Interdependence
13. Tariff
14. European nations
15. World Court
16. Chinese
17. "Asia for the Asiatics"
18. Negroes
19. Revolution
20. Philippine independence[32]

In all of the teacher guides, Rugg and another one of his students, James Mendenhall, included a discussion of 10 psychological principles of learning underpinning the entire program. According to the first principle, the pupil "learns by active assimilation." The keynotes of the "older formal school" were rote learning, order, and attention, they said. Students, Rugg claimed, rarely were asked what they thought about contemporary issues in this stultifying atmosphere. "What does the book say?" was the dominant question of the school day. To Rugg and Mendenhall, restraint and repression in the social studies classroom would be replaced by "guided growth in the ability to reason." As the above list illustrates, the intertwined issues of war and peace were very much a part of the active schooling advocated by Rugg in the workbooks. To reinforce this orientation, Rugg presented students with an opinion survey relating to issues they later would confront in the text. Among the questions in the survey were those dealing with student impressions of the German people, the lessons of World War I, the best way to settle international disputes, and the war guilt problem. Clearly, an attempt was being made to involve the students in thinking "beyond the textbook" about issues that were then and still are controversial.[33]

The 17 social studies generalizations relating to war, colored as they were by the sweeping changes wrought by the collapse of thrones and empires in 1918, constituted an ominous warning for the future when framed in the Rugg curriculum. In one of the workbooks, an eerie cartoon by Hendrick W. Van Loon, in which death was personified as a military drummer leading humanity to a great precipice, reflected Bowman's generalization on the manipulation of public opinion.

Rugg once remarked to his colleagues that "the schools were indeed the chief contestants in the battle between humanitarian international cooperation and selfish nationalism."[34] The 17 generalizations on war and international relations, diplomacy, boundaries, international trade, and imperialism, which Rugg and his research group at Lincoln School integrated into the texts and workbooks of *Man and His Changing Society*, built on the historical friction between these two forces. A look back on the generalizations yields a curious reflection on the legacy left by the Great War to some of the frontier thinkers whose works were published in the 1920s.

Through Wallas's "consciousness of a common purpose in mankind" (598) and Bowman's call for political coordination as a viable alternative to war in the international pursuit for vital economic resources (593), Rugg's drive for world peace through the League of Nations was delivered, a theme prominently expressed in at least three of his textbooks. The influence of Bowman's thought is apparent in the treatment accorded to the Treaty of Versailles, as well as in Rugg's sharp attack on the American government's propaganda activities in galvanizing public opinion. The tensions arising out of the competition for markets and colonies also did not escape Rugg's attention. In his wholehearted support of President Woodrow Wilson's call for open covenants between nations, he included extensive text material on Bryce's observation concerning secret diplomacy, one of the long-term causes of World War I that Rugg especially wished to convey to his young readers.

THE RUGG TEXTBOOK LEGACY

The Rugg series enjoyed a huge success for at least a decade. Between 1929, when the first volume was published by Ginn and Company, and 1939, 1,317,960 copies of the texts and an astounding 2,687,000 copies of the workbooks were sold.[35] Conservative opposition to the series gained some momentum in the late 1930s, and, ironically, America's entry into World War II late in 1941 made Rugg's criticisms of the Great War unpopular and perhaps even irrelevant. The postwar period, dominated as it was by the ill-fated life adjustment movement, marked a return to a social studies curriculum keyed merely to efficient functioning of citizens, much as the early scientific curriculum makers had advocated. An undercurrent of social protest remained but did not enjoy the popularity it achieved in the prewar depression era.

Once life adjustment education collapsed under the withering attack by academicians charging anti-intellectualism in the curriculum, the teaching of the social studies, like other subjects, became more discipline- than problem-oriented, although in 1958 the high school course commonly called Problems of Democracy was accorded James B. Conant's prestigious endorsement in his *American High School Today*. The subsequent work of Edwin Fenton, while deploring the teaching of isolated facts, turned to a search for structure within fields like history as the basis for organizing the curriculum in the social studies, rather than toward generalizations that cut across subject-matter lines. In 1979, Frances Fitzgerald issued a strong indictment of the history textbooks then in use. In particular, she castigated social studies textbook authors for the blandness of their treatment of critical social issues, one of the very problems that Rugg sought to redress in his own textbook series.

One would be tempted to conclude that the Rugg series, including his incorporation of an indictment of causes of war, was merely an aberration in the development of the social studies over the course of the twentieth century. After a brief day in the sun, Rugg's dream of an integration of the social studies around social science generalizations that embodied the thinking of major social critics seems to have evaporated, leaving few vestiges. The fact, however, that Fitzgerald's book received such widespread attention is some indication that there may be a strong residue of sentiment for Rugg's position. The popular perception that so-called pendulum swings do occur in terms of educational ideologies sometimes obscures the fact that no single ideology becomes completely dominant even for a relatively brief period. Fundamental ideological positions, like Rugg's effort to tie the work of the schools to a new social vision, are not so much extinguished as submerged. Just as the Great Depression created a climate conducive to the idea that the social studies should focus on critical social problems, so may new social, economic, and political conditions prompt fresh attention to the question of whether the social studies curriculum should become the forum for the consideration of the great problems that American society faces in the modern world.

BOOKS BY FRONTIER THINKERS CITED

Bowman, Isaiah. *The New World: Problems in Political Geography.* New York: World Book, 1921.

Bryce, James. *Modern Democracies.* New York: Macmillan, 1921.

Ellwood, Charles A. *Sociology and Modern Social Problems.* New York: American Book, 1922.

Ely, Richard T. *Outlines of Economics.* New York: Macmillan, 1920.

Huntington, Ellsworth. *Principles of Human Geography.* New York: Wiley, 1921.

Ross, Edward A. *Principles of Sociology.* New York: Century, 1920.

Semple, Ellen. *Influences of Geographic Environment.* New York: Holt, 1911.

Stearns, Harold, ed., *Civilization in the United States, An Inquiry by Thirty Americans.* New York: Harcourt, Brace, 1922.

Tawney, Richard H. *The Acquisitive Society.* New York: Harcourt Brace, 1920.

Wallas, Graham. *Human Nature in Politics.* London: Constable and Co., 1920.

Webb, Beatrice and Sidney Webb. *Industrial Democracy.* New York: Longmans, Green, 1897.

CHAPTER 6

Fads, Fashions, and Rituals:
The Instability of Curriculum Change

Although many school reforms are nearly universally endorsed on the rhetorical level, they remain the subject of skepticism and cynicism in terms of actual practice. This reputation is not entirely undeserved. Unquestionably, some curriculum reforms are indeed ill-considered in the first place and many of those that make some sense fail to make their way into school practice altogether or are notoriously short-lived if they do. No single explanation of this state of affairs is entirely satisfactory since the phenomenon itself takes different forms in different contexts. What may be eminently plausible in one setting makes little sense in another.

This essay attempts to take a broad look at some of the failures that curriculum reform has undergone over the course of roughly the past century. Four possible explanations for these failures are proposed. One deals with the notion of curriculum as being coterminous with life itself. As such, the course of study has no boundaries. Without a distinct focus, curriculum reform efforts are simply dissipated. A second possible explanation draws on a 1901 address by John Dewey, who, even then, drew attention to the common disjuncture between the rhetoric of reform and the way in which schools are structured. Dewey's perspective on the problem is similar to that taken up some 70 years later by Seymour Sarason, who further explored the significance of that disjuncture. A third possibility takes up the question of the relationship between attempts to change the curriculum in a given direction and the social and political climate of the time. Here too, a disjuncture can become fatal. Finally, there is the way in which the question of curriculum reform is related to the culture of schooling, particularly that of school administration. When the professional culture shifted from a largely intellectual tradition to a bureaucratic one, the process of change took on a new and troublesome direction.

It has become commonplace for observers of the educational landscape, particularly in the field of curriculum, to take note (frequently with alarm) of the short life span of many so-called reforms. Allusions to the phenomenon of "pendulum swings" abound, but relatively little has been adduced as to the reasons for that phenomenon. Cycles occur, of course, in other areas such as politics and clothing fashions, but critics claim that the fads in the curriculum world occur with greater rapidity and that they are often substitutes for genuine and needed change in the system. Moreover, a sense of pessimism often accompanies the articulation of the phenomenon, since there seems to be little point in working for reform when the inevitable result is a return to the status quo. When these cycles become habitual, it is difficult to maintain even the illusion of progress.

I should like to offer four hypotheses that could account for the occurrence of cyclical change in curriculum affairs as it is commonly observed: The first has to do with the almost indefinite expansion of the scope of the curriculum in conjunction with direct utility as the supreme criterion of success. Practically speaking, there are no boundaries to what can be included in the curriculum, and, therefore, any contender is legitimate. Second, because the rhetoric of reform is usually more powerful than that of the opposition, a reform is inaugurated without the accompanying structural changes that are needed in order to make it succeed. When this occurs, the life span of the reform is almost always bound to be short. Third, the changes themselves do not take the form of one curriculum ideology actually displacing another so much as they do a resurfacing of a temporarily submerged position in the light of favorable social and political conditions. Since curriculum ideologies obviously are not independent of the social and political climate, the changes become a function of the interaction of a given social and political climate with certain familiar ideas as to how the curriculum should be selected and organized. And finally, rapid changes in curriculum fashion are related to the rise of a professional class of school administrators, whose professional status and perhaps even survival depend simply on being at least as up-to-date as the school system down the road. In other words, change itself is perceived as desirable rather than change in a particular direction, and, therefore, change tends to be more for the purpose of public display than as the result of firmly held pedagogical beliefs. These four hypotheses are not meant to exhaust the possibilities for explaining the phenomenon of curriculum instability, but they may offer a starting point for a serious investigation of its persistence.

BEYOND ACADEMICS: BUILDING A CURRICULUM FOR "LIFE"

One phenomenon of particular significance regarding the course of study has been its almost indefinite expansion through the twentieth century. In high schools, for example, it is not uncommon for as many as 400 subjects to be offered,[1] with programs added on as critical problems such as instances of adolescent suicide become matters of public concern. Compared with the four sedately academic programs of study recommended by the Committee of Ten in 1893[2] (which itself sanctioned the admission of relatively new subjects, such as modern foreign languages), the modern high school curriculum simply has no boundaries. Covering the span of the entire educational ladder, state departments of education, school boards, and school administrators are continually responding to public outcry, media attention, and pressure from interest groups to include this or that in the curriculum. Moreover, this expansion of the course of study has proceeded at such a pace that it has become almost impossible to speak about *the* American curriculum except in very general terms. As Robert Hampel has pointed out, two major new reports on the state of education in the United States independently called their concluding sections, "We Want It All."[3] The curriculum has become everything but also nothing that can be easily characterized except in those all-inclusive terms. The fine art of *exclusion* in curriculum matters has fallen into wide disfavor.

While this state of affairs is to some extent dictated simply by the absence of purpose in curriculum matters, it is also the culmination of a concerted and self-conscious drive to break down what were considered to be artificial barriers between school and life. With the arrival of mass public education, the academic curricula of the nineteenth century were considered to be simply beyond the mental capacities or irrelevant to the interests of the new population of students entering schools, particularly at the high school level. The basic response to mass public education was to adapt the curriculum to the "needs" of the majority of students, allegedly incapable of profiting from the standard curriculum. Therefore, in the early twentieth century, we begin to see the curriculum modified in an effort to tie the subjects of study more closely to the actual activities that human beings perform. Typical of the reaction to the traditional curriculum was that of the superintendent of schools in the small city of Eau Claire, Wisconsin, one of a new breed of professional school administrators, who declared in 1911 that the "most marked defect" of the curriculum was that it was simply "too bookish and too little related to life and the actual needs of those entering upon the duties of citizenship."[4] And, in fact, he was able to fashion a curriculum by 1915 that was substantially in tune with that sentiment.

Within a relatively few years of the issuance of the Committee of Ten report, major leaders in the newly emerging curriculum field were urging that traditional academic subjects be restricted to a particular group destined for college, with the majority of students engaged in studying subjects that were directly related to their functioning as citizens, as family members, and as workers. One notable example of such an effort was the work of Franklin Bobbitt in bringing such new curriculum ideas to the city of Los Angeles. As a professor on the education faculty of the University of Chicago, Bobbitt was in a position not simply to issue pronouncements on what the curriculum should be like, but to influence practice in cities like Cleveland and San Antonio through his consulting work and through the increasingly fashionable school survey as an instrument for changing the curriculum.

In the case of Los Angeles, Bobbitt actually was employed by the school system for a period of 3 months in order to initiate the curriculum reform project, and it continued, practically speaking, for the entire 1922–23 school year. As a first step, Bobbitt undertook to draw up "a comprehensive list of human abilities and characteristics which appear to be generally needed by the citizens of Los

Angeles."[5] In other words, the curriculum, as Bobbitt envisioned it, was not a collection of subjects deemed to be representative of intellectual culture (as was at least implicitly assumed by the Committee of Ten), but a scientifically determined catalog of actual activities performed by citizens in a given locale. This meant essentially that there simply were no limits to the curriculum except insofar as it coincided with life as it was actually lived. Bobbitt arranged the activities that would form the basis of the curriculum according to his own system of classification:

     I. Social intercommunication, mainly language
    II. The Development and Maintenance of One's Physical Powers
   III. Unspecialized Practical Labors
   IV. The Labors of One's Calling
    V. The Activities of the Efficient Citizen
   VI. Activities Involved in One's General Social Relationships
       and Behavior
  VII. Leisure Occupations, Recreations, Amusements
 VIII. Development and Maintenance of One's Mental Efficiency
   IX. Religious Activities
    X. Parental Activities, the Upbringing of Children, the Maintenance
       of the Home Life[6]

As Bobbitt himself recognized, "There are probably few desirable human activities which will not fall within one or another of these several categories."[7] Moreover, these activities were set forth in minute detail. Included, for example, were "535. Shaving," "551. The boxing, crating, or otherwise making up packages for parcel post or express," and "630. Ability and disposition to earn the equivalent of what one consumes and to share effectively in a public opinion that makes this demand of all. A sense of personal independence that will not permit one to be an economic parasite upon others, and which demands that others be not parasitic upon him." Whatever objections may be raised to Bobbitt's ultimately quixotic attempt to catalog all of human activity or to his smuggling in his own values under the guise of scientifically observed activities, his abiding conviction that the curriculum should be geared to *life* and not mere intellectual mastery remained not only a persistent but a dominant theme in curriculum thinking.

Although the contemporary American curriculum obviously does not reflect precisely the tenets that Bobbitt set forth, it has moved sufficiently in that direction so that there is little sense among school people that a line can be drawn between what is appropriate to include in the curriculum and what is inappropriate. For all intents and purposes, anything goes, and the sheer inclusiveness of what passes for the curriculum in modern times may have a great deal to do with its apparent instability. If the curriculum is to be substantially tied to those things that human beings need to know in order to perform their daily tasks successfully, then as those activities and the perception of the problems of living change, the curriculum must change correspondingly. Curriculum reform, in this sense, represents a never-ending process of making room for an emerging and presumably urgent kind of activity that needs to be performed.

Cast in its most positive light, fads and fashions in curriculum represent merely a process by which the curriculum responds to changing needs and times. But what has been lost in that process is any sense of what a school is for. As John Goodlad, reporting on statements of purpose prepared by the 50 states, commented, "There is something for everyone in the material prepared by the states. But because the documents range over such a variety of topics . . . , one gets little sense of what is essential and what is secondary."[8] Aims stated in terms such as "self realization" and "worthy home membership" function primarily as slogan systems, ritualistic statements that possibly can enlist public support, but in no sense set limits on or give direction to what should be included in the curriculum. If anything, they are a license to do anything. Rather than statements of the purposes of schooling that are laundry lists of high-sounding aims, those purposes should address some sense of priorities in relation to the institutional setting where the purposes are to be accomplished. In part at least, this means a reconsideration of the school as an all-encompassing institution ready and able to accomplish almost anything. It requires hard decisions about the distinctive role of formal schooling in relation to the roles of other social institutions. Such a reconsideration does not mean simply abandoning all other roles; it does mean seeing them as subsidiary to a central one.

Intellectual mastery of the modern world has never been formally rejected as the central purpose of schooling, but in practical terms, it has waxed and waned in terms of both professional and public consciousness. Americans have always had a supreme faith in the power of formal schooling to do many things in addition to initiating youth into the intellectual resources of our culture. Rarely has that faith been examined in realistic terms, and the rise and fall of many so-called innovations may be simply a result of the school's inability to function successfully in terms of such amorphous curriculum boundaries, as well as the kind of direct and concrete payoff that certain curriculum leaders, such as Bobbitt, envisioned. A more appropriate starting point than a catalog of human activity would be to examine seriously and honestly the nature of schooling, not only what it should accomplish in terms of its central task, but what it *can* realistically be expected to do. We would then be in a position to use that conception of schooling as a filter to screen out trivial or chimerical proposals for curriculum change as well as those that are best attempted in another setting. Without disciplined attention to what should be excluded from the curriculum, a revolving door in curriculum matters becomes almost inevitable.

CURRICULUM CHANGE VERSUS ORGANIZATIONAL STRUCTURE

Just as the twentieth century was dawning, John Dewey may have hit upon one of the most significant reasons why curriculum innovations were failing with such monotonous regularity. A change in curriculum is more than it appears to be. It involves not simply the substitution of one element of a course of study for another; that new element frequently requires for its survival a compatible organizational structure. In other words, when a curriculum change is introduced without due regard for modification of the context in which the change is to take place, the innovation is almost surely doomed to a short life. Referring to educational reformers like Horace Mann and Pestalozzi, Dewey argued that their progressive reforms had become commonplace in terms of "pedagogic writing and of the gatherings where teachers meet for inspiration and admonition."[9] The catch was that while the domain of "preaching" had been secured by the reformer, "the conservative, so far as the course of study was concerned, was holding his own pretty obstinately in the region of practice."[10]

In these circumstances, Dewey pointed out, the reforms, when instituted, create "a congestion in the curriculum," which weakens their strength and leads to their being characterized as "fads and frills."[11] When financial troubles occur or when the simple efficiency of the school is somehow impaired, the "insertions and additions" get cast out, precisely because they have not become part of the educational whole.[12] While the reform has the advantage in terms of rhetoric, it becomes inserted into a system that draws its criteria of success from existing standards, a situation that almost ensures that the reform will be temporary. The fact is, as Dewey pointed out, that "we have no conscious educational standard by which to test and place each aspiring claimant. We have hundreds of reasons for and against this or that study, but no reason."[13] An obvious case in point is the persistence of scores on achievement tests as the ultimate criterion of success in curriculum ventures. Certain kinds of success are amenable to that kind of measurement, but others are not. As Dewey expressed it,

> The things of the spirit do not lend themselves easily to that kind of external inspection which goes by the name of examination. They do not lend themselves easily to exact quantitative measurement. Technical proficiency, acquisition of skill and information present much less difficulty. So again emphasis is thrown upon those traditional subjects of the school curriculum which permit most readily of a mechanical treatment—upon the three R's and upon the facts of external classification in history and science, matters of formal technique in music, drawing, and manual training.[14]

Thus, as long as criteria of success that are incompatible with the survival of the reform remain in place, the new program's place in the school curriculum is bound to be short-lived.

2014   the arts

Dewey distinguished between two sorts of studies. The first represents "the symbols of intellectual life, which are the tools of civilization itself." These are the traditional subjects of study. The other group aims at "the direct and present expression of power on the part of one undergoing education, and for the present and direct enrichment of his life-experience."[15] It is the conflict between these two conceptions of the course of study that leads to much of the backing and filling in curriculum affairs. Dewey offered the following proposition as his key to unlocking this conflict:

> The studies of the symbolic and formal sort represented the aids and material of education for a sufficiently long time to call into existence a machinery of administration and of instruction thoroly [*sic*] adapted to themselves. This machinery constituted the actual working scheme of administration and instruction. The conditions this constituted persist long after the studies to which they are well adapted have lost their theoretical supremacy. The conflict, the confusion, the compromise, is not intrinsically between the older group of studies and the newer, but between the external conditions in which the former were realized and the aims and standards represented by the newer.[16]

Seen in this light, curriculum reform exists in a school culture that is basically antagonistic to it. The administrative structure of the school and the modes of teaching that prevail are drawn from another theoretical framework, and the persistence of this "machinery" ultimately crushes curriculum reform. The problem is the basic incompatibility between the structure and organization of the school and the conditions necessary for the success of the reform. We sometimes fall into the trap, Dewey implied, of thinking of such things as sorting children by grade levels and the system of selecting teachers as "matters of mere practical convenience and expediency." Quite the contrary, Dewey argued, "it is precisely such things as these that really control the whole system, even on its distinctively educational side."[17]

Thus, if reformers were to undertake to teach critical or creative or imaginative thinking, for example, they would have to fit that change into an administrative and structural machinery that already has embedded in it the conditions for the downfall of the reform. The new curriculum most likely would be taught as a series of discrete skills, much like reading is, in a setting requiring order and regimentation. And the teachers would be, in all likelihood, instructed merely to carry forward a curriculum in which they had no stake and that they had no part in creating. The teacher, in Dewey's day and in ours, has, by virtue of training and working conditions, no conception of what the curriculum means as a whole, and, as Dewey pointed out, "it is certainly beyond controversy that the success of the teacher in teaching, and of the pupil in learning will depend on the intellectual equipment of the teacher."[18] Thus, as long as the structural conditions conducive to the success of reforms are absent and as long as reformers retain the upper hand in terms of public argument, the familiar ebb and flow of curriculum fashions will continue. In a spirit of exaggerated optimism, or perhaps just wishful thinking, Dewey predicted that "we are now nearing the close of the time of tentative, blind empirical experimentation; that we are close to the opportunity of planning our work on the basis of a coherent philosophy of experience and of the relation of school studies to that experience; that we can accordingly take up steadily and widely the effort of changing school conditions so as to make real the aims that command the assent of intelligence."[19] The persistence of cycles of curriculum change is testimony to the fact that that day has not arrived.

It should be no source of comfort to curriculum reformers that 7 decades after Dewey presented his analysis of the phenomenon, Seymour Sarason arrived at essentially the same explanation. The only way a process of change that takes the form of "delivery of the curriculum" can be successful, Sarason argued, is if the characteristics of the school culture do not adversely affect it. Take, for example, the common observation that "the relation between teacher and pupil is characteristically one in which the teacher asks questions and the pupil gives an answer."[20] When the role of the student is restricted essentially to that form of verbal intercourse, a reform like the teaching of critical thinking is almost necessarily doomed. In that case, the basic framework of classroom discourse simply is not congenial to the way intellectual or critical inquiry proceeds, and the result is a return to the previous state of affairs. As Sarason expressed it, "[A]ny attempt to change a curriculum independent of changing some characteristic institutional feature runs the risk of partial or complete failure."[21]

Perhaps not coincidentally, Sarason took Dewey's own Laboratory School as an example of how the structural features of a school can be modified in order to support educational reform. Of great significance to the operation of Dewey's school was the fact that it was founded on certain basic pedagogical principles that served as the basis not only for the selection of subject matter but for the way in which the school was organized and how the teachers and other school personnel saw their roles within the organizational structure. There was a basic continuity between what the school was trying to accomplish and the day-to-day work of the school personnel. This did not mean, however, that strict rules were set forth for defining what was proper or improper within the confines of the school. Quite the reverse. As Dewey himself expressed this point, "The principles of the school's plan were not intended as definite rules for what was done in school. . . . [T]he 'principles' formed a kind of working hypothesis rather than a fixed program and schedule. Their application was in the hands of the teachers, and this application was in fact equivalent to their development and modification by the teachers."[22]

built-in
reflection

Additionally, there were weekly meetings with teachers, not to discuss administrative issues or discipline problems, but to review the prior week's work. Significantly, the emphasis was not on projection of activities in terms of the next week's lesson plans or on statements of objectives for the future, but on reflection. Specifically, there were frequent discussions on the workaday operation of the school in relation to the theoretical principles that were supposed to guide it. (Obviously, since hardly any schools have guiding theoretical principles—only statements of mushy slogans—this would not be possible on a widespread basis in schools today.) Moreover, a cooperative social reorganization was deliberately fostered, and teachers were encouraged to visit the classrooms of other teachers. Even formal seminar groups were initiated. As Dewey recalled this emphasis on the sharing of experiences, "There was daily and hourly exchange of results of classroom experience,"[23] exchanges that could be possible only with the conscious modification of the traditional school structure that isolates teachers not only physically by classroom but often by department and by subject. Reports by the teachers formed the basis of the weekly informal conferences, as well as of formal seminar groups. At one teachers' meeting led by Dewey in 1899, a typical question raised was the following:

> Is there any common denominator in the teaching process? Here are people teaching children of different ages, different subjects; one is teaching music, another art, another cooking, Latin, etc. Now is there any common end which can be stated which is common to all? This is meant in an intellectual rather than a moral way. Is there any intellectual result which ought to be obtained in all these different studies and at these different ages?[24]

The weekly meetings on *pedagogical* questions were one element of an organizational structure designed to be consistent with the working hypothesis that was the theoretical basis of the school.

As Sarason pointed out, "John Dewey created a school; he did not have to change an ongoing one."[25] Oddly enough, it may be a less formidable task to create a new institution than to effect structural changes in an existing one. Dewey's followers, just like many modern reformers, set out to carry forward the ideals that guided the Laboratory School to a wider spectrum of schools. But ideas and "missionary zeal" are not sufficient conditions to bring about real change.[26] As Dewey observed at the turn of the twentieth century, the rhetorical battle may be won in those circumstances, but lasting reform cannot be. The machinery of the organization and its internal dynamics must be changed accordingly if the innovation is to have any chance of succeeding. This requires an intimate understanding of the particular institutional culture involved, not a putative generalized formula for how to succeed.

CURRICULUM CHANGE, THE POLITICAL MOOD, AND SOCIAL PROGRESS

Americans have such an abiding faith in the power of education to effect both fundamental social change and alterations in basic human values that they need to be reminded every now and then that formal education does not exist independent of its relationship to the larger social order and to other sources of human action. Their belief in education is so strong that it is widely regarded as the most efficacious instrument of social progress. When a major problem of almost any sort arises, ranging from an AIDS epidemic to large-scale unemployment, Americans characteristically look to schools as the way to address it. As Henry Steele Commager once put it, "In the past we required our schools to do what in the Old World the family, the church, apprenticeship and the guilds did; now we ask them to do what their modern equivalents, plus a hundred voluntary organizations, fail or refuse to do."[27] This exaggerated faith in the power of one social institution to accomplish almost anything, especially without due regard for other social forces and institutions, may itself be one factor contributing to the parade of curriculum fashions. When schools blithely undertake, or have thrust upon them, a function for which they are unsuited, then the program collapses of its own weight, only to be replaced by another one when the national mood changes.

This is not to say that schools and programs of study in schools are mere reflections of larger social forces over which the schools have no control. It does mean that ideas about what should be taught in school, rather than being independent of those forces, are in constant interaction with social trends. But it is not the actual events or trends themselves that are the sources of the curriculum cycles. It is the events or trends as filtered through certain fundamental beliefs about the nature and function of the curriculum that pervade our consciousness. Robert Nisbet expressed the basic idea most cogently: "We may think we are responding directly to events and changes in the history of institutions, but we aren't; we are responding to these events and changes as they are made real or assimilable to us by ideas already in our heads."[28] If some kind of understanding of the cycles of curriculum fashion is to be achieved, then, it is likely that we would have to come to grips with the question of how events in the larger social and political sphere interact with fundamental ideas we have about what should be taught in schools.

Perhaps a couple of examples can illustrate this point. As World War II was drawing to a close, there was a natural tendency for Americans to yearn for "normalcy." The reaction to the disruption and turmoil that the war effort had created made the appeal of a society that ran smoothly and where people adjusted contentedly to their roles in the social order particularly potent. That national mood interacted with the curriculum doctrine that held out the most promise for achieving that state of normalcy—social efficiency. Ever since that doctrine had emerged

birth of adjustment
"life adjustment clinic"
🅐

in a coherent form just after the turn of the twentieth century, its appeal had been to those who sought a stable social order that simply worked efficiently. The postwar national mood in interaction with social efficiency as a curriculum idea emerged in the mid-1940s as life adjustment education. The enormous appeal of life adjustment education to educational leaders and school personnel across the country was its promise of the harmonious adjustment of American citizens to what life had in store for them. When conflict re-emerged only a few years later in the form of the Cold War, life adjustment education quickly fell out of fashion. The new national mood was one of fierce competition with the Soviet Union, especially in the areas of science and technology. Interacting with that national mood were curriculum ideas that stressed tough academics and strenuous mental activity. What emerged, especially after Sputnik punctuated the process that was already taking place, was a radically different curriculum doctrine whose major emphasis was on the structure of the various academic disciplines. That "cycle" then moved from a "soft" education emphasizing learning the everyday tasks of life as the route to happy adjustment, to a "hard" education emphasizing academic rigor as a way coming to grips with a serious external threat. But it was dictated neither by a social trend nor by a curriculum doctrine alone; it was the result of a perceived problem interacting with an extant curriculum doctrine. In Nisbet's terms, these events were made real by ideas that were already floating around in our heads.

If we pursue further, however, the case of the public reaction to Sputnik, it is also illustrative of the peculiarly American tendency to look to schools as the corrective for major social or political or even technological deficiencies. Although the "soft" American curriculum provided a convenient and perhaps even publicly plausible way of explaining the Soviet Union's accomplishment in space technology, the actual reasons for their success in sending a satellite into orbit in 1957 were undoubtedly much more complex than and perhaps even irrelevant to the question of whether schools in America taught less of this or more of that than Soviet schools did. It is in this sense that the Sputnik experience is also illustrative of the characteristic tendency of Americans to exaggerate the power of formal schooling to correct social deficiencies and to act as a direct instrument of progress. The relationship, then, between national trends as they affect curriculum policy on one hand and the supreme faith of Americans in the sheer power of education as a force for progress on the other makes changes in curriculum fashion a naturally recurring phenomenon. As long as public concern about various social tendencies continues to shift and as long as schooling is seen as the way to alleviate that concern, then curriculum doctrine will shift as well.

Although this state of affairs may be inevitable under present conditions, it cannot be a source of satisfaction either with respect to the conduct of schooling or as a way of achieving social progress. No one can be against progress, but genuine progress actually can be impeded when it is equated with mere change and especially when it is only the appearance of change. In the first place, change alone can be regressive as well as progressive. This is embedded in the "pendulum swing" metaphor commonly used to describe the phenomenon. Second, as Commager's felicitous characterization, "the school as surrogate conscience," implies,[29] attributing critical social responsibilities to schools may turn out simply to be a way of avoiding the stark realities of the situation. Merely assigning schools the responsibility for addressing problems not only of a perceived space race, but of alcoholism, drug addiction, teenage pregnancy, or poverty, may serve to salve the public conscience; in the long run, however, it also may serve to impair genuine attempts to address those issues with all the seriousness they deserve.

CHANGING FASHIONS AND THE CULTURE OF PROFESSIONAL SCHOOL ADMINISTRATION

Just as one can speak of an institution as having a distinctive culture, so may one at least raise the question of whether a professional field can be similarly characterized. Tyack and Hansot, for example, have argued that a temper of millennialism and a crusading spirit drawn from an early-nineteenth-century Protestant ethic continued to animate the work of school administrators even after the industrial revolution transformed the material conditions of schooling.[30] But while some residue of that spirit may have survived into the twentieth century, there also was developing a new culture of educational administration that was tied more closely to professional expertise than to traditional Protestant values.

Beginning roughly in the 1890s, the model for the aspiring as well as the established school administrator shifted from Protestant revivalism to bureaucratic efficiency. In effect, this new professionalism ultimately evolved into what Tyack and Hansot call an "educational trust."[31] A federation of tightly knit networks not only dominated the day-to-day operations of public schools for at least most of the twentieth century, but also spread the gospel of the new management practices that were to provide America's public schools with the metaphors and the standards of success that set the tone for what constituted an up-to-date curriculum.[32] Typical of the new way of thinking about schooling in general and the curriculum in particular was the following from the work of one of the key members of the school administration trust, Ellwood P. Cubberley of Stanford University:

> Every manufacturing establishment that turns out a standard product or a series of products of any kind maintains a force of efficiency experts to study methods of procedure and to measure and test the output of its works. Such men ultimately bring the manufacturing establishment large returns by introducing improvements in processes and procedure, and in training the workmen to produce larger and better out-

put. Our schools are, in a sense, factories in which the raw products (children) are to
be shaped and fashioned into products to meet the various demands of life. The specifications for manufacturing come from the demands of twentieth-century civilization, and it is the business of the school to build its pupils according to the specifications laid down. This demands good tools, specialized machinery, continuous
measurement of production to see if it is according to specifications, and a large variety
in the output.[33]

Given the power and influence of the school administration trust, intellectual credentials were quickly replaced as the basis for heading a school or a school system by professional credentials that included not only a degree in administration
but an ideology drawn from the world of business and manufacturing.

   Two powerful mechanisms helped spread the message of a needed change
in school practices: One was the school survey (of which Cubberley's Portland
survey is a prime example). Typically, a school system would invite a member of
the trust, such as Cubberley or George Strayer of Teachers College, to conduct a
survey of the school system's program of studies. Almost invariably the survey
report would include recommendations for needed changes, and to demonstrate
that the school system was in step with the latest trends, local school officials had
almost no recourse but to try to implement those recommendations. The second
mechanism comprised a system of private networks established by prominent
leaders in the burgeoning field of school administration, which ensured that only
those with the right ideas occupied key superintendencies. Perhaps the most natural
network consisted simply of the students trained by one of the leaders. According
to Tyack and Hansot, for example, Strayer's influence was significant not only in
terms of what he taught in his courses at Teachers College, but "in his role as a
placement baron" as well.[34] As they explained the relationship,

> The relation between sponsor and alumnus was one of mutual advantage. In return
> for assistance in moving ahead on the chessboard of superintendencies, the alumnus
> helped the professor recruit students, invited the sponsor to consult or survey his
> district, notified him of vacancies, helped place his graduates, and kept him in touch
> with his field. The graduate turned to the sponsor for advice and help in getting ahead.
> His advancement often depended on pleasing his sponsor as well as the local school
> board (of course the two were connected).[35]

It was not long before these mutually advantageous networks began to exhibit their
own norms and behavioral regularities.

   Apart from a generalized business orientation, however, the ideologies were
neither well defined nor internally consistent. According to Tyack and Hansot,
the new breed of school administrators "tended to have prefabricated solutions to
preconceived problems. One reason for this was that they did not inquire in any

fundamental or open-minded way into the conflicting goals of education. . . ."[36]
The overarching motive for instituting any change was to demonstrate that one's
own school system was at least as innovative as others in the vicinity. Without
any sense of purpose or deeply held commitments to a particular course of action (except perhaps to hard efficiency), change itself became a predominant
factor in the emerging culture of school administration. No administrator could
really afford to stand pat. And when change occurs simply for the sake of change,
it is no great mystery as to why changes in schools occur and recur with such
monotonous regularity. Survival, or at least status, for the school administrator
came to depend on change alone, not on change in a particular direction.

FOUR HYPOTHESES REVIEWED

There can be no single-factor explanation for so broad and widespread a phenomenon as the constant ebb and flow of curriculum fashions. It is likely that
such a persistent pattern is an outgrowth of plural causes and tendencies. Among
some of the more plausible of these are the four factors outlined here.

The first relates to the absence of purpose in curriculum decision making,
a lack that has opened the door for virtually any candidate to be admitted to
the course of study. In an age when an academic curriculum prevailed, for
example, certain subjects were out of bounds or at least subsidiary. In the
age of a "shopping mall" curriculum, nothing can be excluded, and this
dictates the perennial shift of what the curriculum is in any given time and place.
As long as the boundaries of the curriculum are conterminous with the boundaries of life, "social skills" can enjoy equal status with biology as a school
subject.

The second is a function of a basic incompatibility between the rhetoric of
school reform and the way in which schools are organized. In these circumstances,
innovations that win the battle of words prove indigestible within the supremely
stable structure of schooling and ultimately are regurgitated. Only when the significance of the institutional culture is recognized as a vital factor in curriculum
reform can change be sustained.

Third, the combination of a supreme faith in the power of schooling and the
interactive relationship between curriculum ideas and political and social trends
also contributes to the pattern of cycles. As new social tendencies emerge, they
become real (in school terms) by being filtered through certain fundamental ideas
about curriculum, and as different social tendencies resonate with different curriculum ideologies, one curriculum fashion supplants another. Unfortunately, this
process takes place almost unconsciously and without due cognizance of the implications of those fundamental ideas.

The fourth hypothesis is related to the fact that day-to-day decision making in the schools of America is, by and large, in the hands of a professional breed of school administrators who have been socialized into a particular way of thinking and acting. Over the course of the twentieth century, the culture of school administration has drawn extensively from the canons and culture of the business world. Without an articulated sense of inquiry into the nature and purposes of schooling, that professional culture encourages not change in a purposive direction, but change itself.

CHAPTER 7

Cultural Literacy, or The Curate's Egg

The validity of at least one of the assumptions that E. D. Hirsch sets forth appears to be undeniable. The general knowledge of the youth of the nation has declined over the course of years. That this state of affairs is so widely recognized probably accounts at least in part for the enormous success of Hirsch's provocative book. Not only did Cultural Literacy *stay at the top of the best-seller lists for many weeks; it also spawned several elaborations on the subject and a series of works setting standards for achieving cultural literacy at various grade levels. Hirsch also was probably correct in arguing that a lack of cultural literacy can have damaging consequences in terms of social relations and life chances. The fact that Hirsch argues persuasively about the decline of general knowledge and its negative consequences, however, does not necessarily lend credibility to his analysis of the source of the problem nor does it mean that his proposed solution to it has any validity.*

Many of the drawbacks to Hirsch's solution are rooted in his faulty analysis of the causes of the problem. He assumes, for example, that the kinds of things he includes in his long list of components of cultural literacy are simply not taught in schools. It is very difficult, however, to posit any generalizations about the American curriculum because it is determined largely by thousands of individual school districts. Surely no school undertakes to teach all of the items on Hirsch's list or even most of them, but anyone who has had experience teaching in American schools can attest to the fact that many of them do make their way into the typical course of study, either formally or informally. The dates of the Civil War, to take one example from Hirsch's list, are nearly universally taught. The fact that many American college students cannot even identify the half-century in which that war took place, much less the exact dates, does not mean that they have not been taught those dates; it means that they have consciously or unconsciously rejected that knowledge. It is surely difficult to pinpoint the exact reasons for that rejection, but it most certainly has nothing to do with the philosophy of John Dewey, as Hirsch contends. My own hunch is that having grown up in a money culture, most American youth have become socialized into thinking that the main purpose of schooling, virtually the only one, has to do with making a living and, therefore, the dates of the American Civil War are simply beside the point.[1]

The rather strange title of this essay is intended to convey the way I resolved my own ambivalence about Hirsch's proposal for reforming the curriculum. Although I am sympathetic to resolving the dilemma that he identifies, and I share his sense of frustration, I cannot accept the solution he offers. His faulty analysis makes the whole egg smell bad. I also admit to a certain playfulness in throwing out my own bit of cultural literacy. Admittedly, "curate's egg" is more obscure than quite a few of the items that found their way onto Hirsch's long list but, like his "carrying coals to Newcastle," it is one more tiny shard of cultural literacy nevertheless.

Right Reverend Host: "I'm afraid you've got a bad egg, Mr. Jones!"
The Curate: "Oh no, my Lord, I assure you! Parts of it are excellent!"[2]

As with almost any policy proposal, one usually can separate the parts that seem to make sense from those that are open to question. But in the case of E. D. Hirsch, Jr.'s *Cultural Literacy: What Every American Needs to Know*,[3] the problem is one of whether it is at all possible to sort out the ingredients in such a way as to salvage what is valid and agreeable from what is plainly repugnant and offensive. Like all good academicians, Hirsch is in favor of excellence and opposed to anti-intellectualism in schools, but his idiosyncratic version of what excellence means and his seriously flawed interpretation of the failings of American schooling as well as the sources of these problems makes his position especially difficult to disentangle. In the end, it comes down to the question of whether Hirsch's conception of cultural literacy, like the curate's egg, can be judged partly good and partly bad. The curate's circumspect verdict notwithstanding, Hirsch appears to have served up an egg that may have to be judged, like eggs in general, not in terms of its parts but as a whole.

First, let it be said that Hirsch raises the most profound of curriculum issues. Whatever else it is, the curriculum is a selection of the elements of a culture. Questions such as what should be selected, how this selection from the resources of a culture ought to be accomplished, by whom, using what criteria, and with what effect, form the basis of what it means to study the curriculum. At the very least, therefore, Hirsch deserves credit for stimulating public discussion on these most central questions. The question of why Americans are ignorant of certain matters that we take to be fundamental, or that we regard as relatively commonplace elements of our culture, deserves serious examination. Hirsch, however, makes a wholly inadequate case as to the sources of the problem and proposes a course of action that is potentially disastrous for educational practice.

There seems to be no question that at least one of Hirsch's basic assumptions is a valid one. Literacy does not consist of simply encoding written symbols. To be literate at all is to attach meaning to those symbols. Based on that assumption, Hirsch goes on to draw the inference (actually in his opening sentence) that "[t]o be culturally literate is to possess the basic information needed to thrive in the modern world."[4] Cultural literacy, therefore, is defined not as a complex system of shared meanings, values, beliefs, and ways of thinking, but as a fund of items of "information." Moreover, it is this information that is necessary for any member of the society to "thrive," that is, to grow and prosper. From this definition of what cultural literacy consists of, Hirsch proceeds in what is probably the most controversial part of his thesis to actually enumerate several thousand of the components that constitute cultural literacy. The list is an alphabetically organized conglomeration that includes (but is not restricted to) a few dates (1066, 1492, 1861–1865), a seemingly miscellaneous selection of Latin or other foreign terms used in English (*annus mirabilis*, Rosh Hashanah, zeitgeist), some geographic locations (Rio de Janeiro; Newark, New Jersey; Liverpool), an odd collection of the names of literary, historical, and sports figures (Nathaniel Hawthorne, J. Edgar Hoover, Jesse Owens), a sprinkling of scientific terms (meiosis, RNA, ribonucleic acid), some seemingly random expressions (Rome wasn't built in a day; steal one's thunder; Tom, Dick, and Harry), a dash of names drawn from classical mythology (Hymen, Minerva, Poseidon), and the titles of a few literary works (*Tobacco Road, The Great Gatsby, Pilgrim's Progress*). Hirsch concedes that his list of roughly 4,000 to 5,000 items is incomplete, and he invites his readers to submit comments and additions. He reminds his correspondents, however, that he actually is not trying to create a complete catalog of American knowledge, "but to establish guideposts that can be of practical use to teachers, students, and all others who need to know our literate culture."[5] I suppose we should take Hirsch at his word, but it seems that if "guideposts" were really the purpose, then a dozen or two examples would have sufficed, and he would not have required the assistance of two distinguished collaborators in creating the list, Joseph Kett, a historian, and James Trefil, a physicist, as well as more than 100 consultants. And what would be the purpose of holding out the promise of an as-yet-undefined expansion of the list? Hirsch's disclaimer notwithstanding, the list looks very much like what the subtitle of his book proclaims, "What Every American Needs to Know."

HOW DID AMERICAN SCHOOLS GET SO BAD?

Hirsch has a story to tell to go with his proposal, a story that presumably accounts for the fact that schools have failed to convey the version of cultural literacy that he propounds. It is supposed to tell us why American schools have devoted themselves in modern times to a vague and intangible thing called *process* and have correspondingly ignored content, the very items of information that make up Hirsch's list. The result is that many graduates of American schools would fail to identify correctly the terms that appear there. This fundamentally flawed account of the sources of the problem constitutes one of the major weaknesses of Hirsch's thesis.

Hirsch's story begins with, of all people, Jean Jacques Rousseau, whose ideas, he audaciously proclaims, "have dominated American education for the past fifty years."[6] The claim, in other words, is that roughly between 1937 and 1987, Rousseau's ideas about "the natural development of young children," including his alleged reluctance to impose adult ideas on the growing child, was a guiding principle in American schools. There is no genuine documentation for such a claim in Hirsch's story, nor could there be because the evidence that exists as to what was taught in American schools during that period runs contrary to what Hirsch asserts. It is true that, here and there, Rousseau found a disciple among American educators (G. Stanley Hall, for example), but there is little evidence that those ideas actually reached the classrooms of the country to any appreciable degree, even around the turn of the twentieth century, when Hall's influence was the strongest. Moreover, as the twentieth century progressed, whatever romantic ideas of childhood had gained a foothold went into a sharp decline. Perhaps the only tangible evidence of something that could be called a child-centered education existed in a handful of upper-middle-class private schools and isolated experimental schools such as Marietta Johnson's in Fairhope, Alabama. It is true that one probably can trace a gradual diminution of emphasis on the academic side of the American curriculum over the course of the twentieth century, but that had little or nothing to do with Rousseau or his disciples. It is much more attributable to a mood of hard-edged efficiency that dominated educational thinking over that period, arising from the impact of industrialism,[7] as well as a growing emphasis on the use of the schools as a direct instrument of social control.[8] Both tendencies are actually virtual antitheses to what Rousseau advocated.

There is more to Hirsch's story. It turns out that the real villain in the piece is none other than John Dewey because, first of all, "Rousseau's ideas powerfully influenced the educational conceptions of John Dewey," and second, Dewey was the person who "most deeply affected modern American theory and practice."[9] These are two additional unfounded allegations, which, like Hirsch's assertions about Rousseau's own purportedly profound influence on the American curriculum, need some unraveling. It is true that Dewey has become a kind of symbol of American education, but beyond the symbolism and the slogans that still are sometimes voiced in his name, one can find almost nothing in American school practice of the educational ideas that Dewey propounded over the course of his long life. There is obviously a huge difference between fame or name recognition on one hand and genuine influence on the other, and it would be a formidable task to find any of Dewey's important ideas on curriculum actually being practiced in American schools.

Hirsch's historical justification for his claim that Rousseau "powerfully influenced" Dewey's ideas on education rests almost exclusively on his reading of only one of Dewey's books. He asserts that Dewey's "clearest . . . and most widely read book on education, *Schools of To-morrow*, acknowledges Rousseau as the chief source of his educational principles."[10] That claim is patently untrue. Dewey never acknowledged any such thing in *Schools of To-morrow* or anywhere else. Dewey and Rousseau had widely divergent views of what constitutes a good education, and that is a matter of record. (There is also good reason to doubt that *Schools of To-morrow* should rank above, say, *School and Society*, *The Child and the Curriculum*, *Democracy and Education*, or *Experience and Education* as Dewey's "most widely read" book on education, but let's not belabor that point.) What is important is what kind of book *Schools of To-morrow* was and whether

Hirsch's bald declaration that it reveals Rousseau's powerful influence on Dewey actually is borne out in the text. First, it should be said that *Schools of To-morrow* was a collaboration between Dewey and his daughter, Evelyn. Dewey states in the preface that "[t]he visiting of the schools with one exception was done by Miss Dewey, who is also responsible for the descriptive chapters in the book."[11] He also reports that the book consists of a kind of catalog of schools that in 1915 were regarded as somehow experimental. The book is basically a piece of reporting. The question must be raised, therefore, as to whether Dewey's ideas on education are best represented in a work where someone else (albeit a close relative) has done most of the writing and that is admittedly a journalistic endeavor.

More important, Dewey asserts in the preface (which is signed J. D.) that the book reviews a variety of theories about education as they are being put into practice in American schools. He states, "It is the function of this book to point out how the applications arise from their theories and the direction that education in this country seems to be taking at the present time."[12] It is hard to imagine that Hirsch, having read those words, could interpret the content of the book as Dewey's "clearest" expression of his own educational ideals, especially since, just in case the point was lost on his readers, Dewey goes on to assert that "[t]he schools that are used for illustration were chosen more or less at random; because we already knew of them or because they were conveniently located."[13] It should be recalled that Hirsch's evidence for Rousseau's "profound" influence on Dewey rests on what Hirsch claims to have gleaned from *Schools of To-morrow*.

It happens that the first chapter of *Schools of To-morrow* is entitled "Education as Natural Development" and is intended to introduce the next chapter, which reports on Marietta Johnson's Fairhope, Alabama, school, a school presumably based on Rousseauian principles. That first chapter, since it not a descriptive account of a particular school but a short review of certain basic ideas that Rousseau held about education, probably was written by John rather than Evelyn Dewey and, therefore, may be instructive as to the extent to which Dewey was "powerfully influenced" by Rousseau, as Hirsch claims. The task is to disentangle what Dewey reported as Rousseau's beliefs on education as a basis for introducing the next chapter from his own judgment about those beliefs. One sentence, for example, unequivocally represents Dewey's own position as opposed to merely summarizing Rousseau's: "Rousseau said, as well as did, many foolish things."[14] Simply put, those words do not sound like those of a true disciple. Here and there, Dewey characteristically says something complimentary about Rousseau. He says, for example, that Rousseau was "far ahead . . . of the psychology of his own day in his conception of the relation of the senses to knowledge."[15] But it is Dewey's last paragraph on the subject of Rousseau's philosophy of education that must have set Hirsch's juices flowing. He quotes Rousseau as characterizing information when considered "*as an end in itself*" as an "unfathomable and shoreless ocean" and appears to agree with Rousseau that it is absurd to identify education with the mere accumulation of knowledge. He goes on to associate this with the common practice of equating education with "a smattering and superficial impression of a large and miscellaneous number of subjects . . ." and proposes that, rather than trying to lay out all of knowledge as an educational aim, we ought to concentrate on how "to master the tools of learning."[16] That last statement, of course, would run contrary to the idea of equating education with the mastery of a list of several thousand terms, but, surely, Hirsch would not argue that merely mastering a miscellaneous fund of information should become the end of education. Or would he?

Beyond those few instances of editorializing, Dewey seems to have gone out of his way to make sure that the practices reported in *Schools of To-morrow* did not carry his own endorsement. In the first sentence of the concluding chapter, for example, Dewey (most likely John rather than Evelyn) stated unequivocally, "The schools that have been described were selected not because of any conviction that they represent the best work that is being done in this country, *but simply because they illustrate the general trend of education at the present time, and because they seem fairly representative of different types of schools.*"[17] Dewey may have been wrong as to whether all the schools described in the book represented a "general trend," but there is no doubt at all that, whatever else it is, *Schools of To-morrow* is not an expression of Dewey's own philosophy of education.

This is all very puzzling. Hirsch is, after all, a scholar of considerable eminence. How could he have been led so far astray in trying to account for the sad state of American schooling? Choosing *Schools of To-morrow* as Dewey's quintessential expression of his philosophical ideas is a blunder one would not expect from someone of Hirsch's stature. One possible explanation is that *Schools of To-morrow* is one of the few places where Dewey had anything at all to say about Rousseau, and Hirsch's fable needed a veneer of plausibility. (The earliest and most profound influence on Dewey's philosophy was Hegel.[18]) One can only speculate, but it seems likely that Hirsch's passion on this subject simply led him to abandon temporarily his usual scholarly caution, a phenomenon not unknown when academic blood begins to boil on the question of why American youth reject the culture that schools purvey and where the villains responsible have to be exposed and held to account. Even Hirsch's characterization of Rousseau's philosophy of education seems to be based more on popular misconceptions than serious analysis.

TWO HISTORICAL REPORTS CONTRASTED

Hirsch's other forays into historical explanations for the state of American education are almost equally unconvincing, although here and there he does make an important point. He attributes the contemporary fragmentation in the curriculum to two "decisive moments" in the course of American education,[19] the *Report of the Committee on Secondary School Studies* (1893) and the *Cardinal Principles of Secondary Education* (1918). It is always hazardous to attribute historical courses of action to very specific incidents or events, since actually they so rarely initiate long-term trends. In the case of what passes for the American curriculum, its evolution to its present state in all likelihood would have occurred even if those two reports had never existed. But the reports are instructive in illustrating certain competing conceptions of secondary education that were prominent in the late nineteenth and early twentieth centuries. The Committee of Ten, of course, sought to uphold the traditional humanistic curriculum (with some reforms introduced) against the onslaught of a materialistic culture on one hand and an impending influx of a massive new population of students in secondary schools on the other. The *Cardinal Principles*, Hirsch correctly reports, stressed "utility and the direct application of knowledge" primarily for the purpose of "producing good, productive, and happy citizens,"[20] pointing out that the familiar formulation of its seven aims is attuned much more to "social adjustment" than to academic mastery. This characterization of *Cardinal Principles* is accurate enough, but it also should be remembered that Dewey remained all his life unalterably opposed to social adjustment as an aim of education. In fact, social efficiency, the predominant doctrine underlying *Cardinal Principles*, was characterized by Dewey as precisely the opposing position to Rousseau's natural development. That "opposing emphasis," Dewey says in *Democracy and Education*, "took the form of a doctrine that the business of education is to supply precisely what nature fails to secure; namely habituation of an individual to social control; subordination of natural powers to social rules."[21] Hirsch is accusing Dewey, then, at one and the same time of supporting two conflicting educational doctrines, neither of which Dewey in fact supported, and which Dewey recognized as being in opposition to each other.

Instead of entering into a serious analysis of the origins of the conception of the purposes of secondary education that *Cardinal Principles* embodied, Hirsch chooses to go back to his bête noire theme, with Dewey, of course, as the source of these ideas, and to reiterate the profound misconception that "Dewey was a disciple of Rousseau."[22] To clear up Hirsch's misconceptions about the sources of the ideas that were embodied in *Cardinal Principles* would require a very substantial reexamination of the social and educational conditions under which they were promulgated, but at least a few points should be made for the record. First, Dewey is not mentioned or cited anywhere in *Cardinal Principles*. Second, if there was a single direct influence on the chief architect of the report, Clarence Kingsley, it was one of social efficiency's major champions and Kingsley's mentor, David Snedden, with whom Dewey had an open and rather bitter dispute on the functions of education. Finally, if one had to choose a European source for the ideas that found their way into *Cardinal Principles*, it was certainly not Rousseau or, for heaven's sake, Wordsworth, as Hirsch claims, but Herbert Spencer.

These profound misconceptions aside, Hirsch has something important to say about the differences in outlook between the Committee of Ten report and *Cardinal Principles*. He is certainly incorrect in saying that the earlier committee "rejected as unfeasible" universal secondary education, but to his credit he does point out that there is a sense in which "the earlier document was more egalitarian than the latter."[23] This is a position that runs contrary to much modern sentiment on the subject. The conventional interpretation of the Committee of Ten report sees it as an elitist proposal designed to perpetuate college domination of the high school curriculum and to preserve an archaic academic curriculum in the face of the necessities of mass public education. But Hirsch is on solid ground if he sees Charles W. Eliot and his colleagues on the committee as expressing a faith that popular education does not necessitate a diminished emphasis on the finest intellectual resources of our culture. Eliot was an optimist about human intellectual capacities, and if something can be salvaged from Hirsch's half-hearted foray into historical interpretation of the current state of affairs in education, it is that that faith quickly fell into disrepute under the influence of such powerful figures as Snedden and E. L. Thorndike, and it was their views that tended to predominate, even though they were not uncontested. As Hirsch notes, *Cardinal Principles*, by contrast, did argue for a more utilitarian education. The motivation for that argument, however, was not principally any sentimental concern about the natural development of children (although something of that language tends to creep into almost any educational proposal) but a desire to make education a direct instrument of social efficiency, including, of course, vocational competence. Yes, American education did take a turn at the beginning of the twentieth century and much of it was anti-academic in direction. That course may be legitimately regretted, but Rousseau had nothing to do with it. Dewey, for his part, actually opposed the ideas that were most central to *Cardinal Principles*.

It would be instructive, however, in explaining the decline of the academic emphasis in American education, to contrast Hirsch's finger pointing with Christopher Lasch's discerning analysis.[24] First of all, Lasch is astute enough to understand that "the decline of literacy cannot be attributed solely to the failure of the educational system."[25] In fact, the heart of his analysis rests on the transformation of American culture in modern industrial society. An advanced industrial society, he argues, "no longer rests on a population primed for achievement. It requires a stupefied population, resigned to work that is trivial and shoddily performed, predisposed to seek its satisfaction in the time set aside for leisure."[26] If anything, it is this "spread of stupefaction" as a function of the needs of an industrial society that accounts for the neglect of Dewey's long-standing emphasis on the school's role as the center of intellectual development. It is true that slogans such as the "whole child" were bandied about as the principal reason for the transformation of the American curriculum (and indeed that slogan has had a deleterious effect), but the introduction of homemaking and other nonacademic subjects into the twentieth-century curriculum, Lasch argues, was also a consequence of "the practical need to fill up the students' time and to keep them reasonably contented."[27] As the twentieth century progressed, social efficiency, including its anti-academic emphasis, tended to gain prominence as an educational doctrine because its principal tenets meshed neatly with the demands of modern industrial America.

Like Hirsch, Lasch deplores the branding of academic learning as a kind of elitism. Sharply differentiating the curriculum on the basis of allegedly massive differences in intelligence within the school population, or, worse still, on the basis of a prognostication as to one's future social role, only serves to perpetuate social inequality. "In the long run," Lasch says, "it does not matter to the victims whether bad teaching justifies itself on the reactionary grounds that poor people cannot hope to master the intricacies of mathematics, logic, and English composition or whether, on the other hand, pseudoradicals condemn academic standards as part of the apparatus of white cultural control, which purportedly prevents blacks and other minorities from realizing their creative potential."[28] As long as academic excellence is identified with elitism, the result is the same. On this point, Hirsch and Lasch may share some common ground, but they differ considerably on a definition of a good academic curriculum. A lack of fundamental information is only a small part of what Lasch regards as the failure of mass education.

Hirsch is at his best when he speaks to the question of the origins of national languages and the evolution of literate traditions. He acknowledges the importance of minority cultures but continually returns to his main theme of a broadly American culture. He argues very persuasively for the position that "every national language is a conscious construct that transcends any particular dialect, region, or social class."[29] For Hirsch, the existence of diverse political and cultural values makes the vocabulary of public discourse all the more significant. It provides us with the language by which disputes may be resolved or at least addressed. By language, however, Hirsch does not mean vocabulary in the ordinary sense of the term. He means a "whole system of widely shared information and associations."[30] To regard that system of information and communication as class culture, Hirsch would argue, is a "facile oversimplification,"[31] and I think he is correct in contending that American education, by and large, has not succeeded in purveying the culture that we tend to associate with educated persons. Hirsch, here, is on familiar and solid ground (although I think he is mistaken if he is implying that the educational policy of bilingualism has as its purpose the encouragement of "competing languages within our borders"[32]). In the long run, though, it is his explanation for the failure of schools to educate, along with the recommendations he makes for its correction, that are open to serious question. When the analysis of the problem is seriously flawed, then the recommendations for its resolution are bound to be misguided. They are part of the same egg.

EXORCISING THE DEMON OF FORMALISTIC THEORY

Apart from his historical explanations, Hirsch draws on at least one contemporary study on American schooling to further his argument. He cites the excellent
account of American secondary education presented by Arthur Powell, Eleanor
Farrar, and David Cohen.[33] If the fragmentation of the curriculum that is depicted
in *The Shopping Mall High School* (which Hirsch summarizes briefly) is a basically valid one, and I think it is, then it is in direct opposition to the kind of cohe-
siveness and unity that Dewey strove to embody in the American curriculum.
Hirsch obviously has read *Shopping Mall* since his brief characterization of its
major themes is reasonably accurate,[34] but it is hard to imagine that he has read
Dewey's work on curriculum; the curriculum described in *Shopping Mall*
and Dewey's conception of an ideal curriculum are quite simply irreconcilable.
Hirsch's reading of *Shopping Mall*, however, has led him to the conclusion that
there is a "formalistic theory" (presumably Dewey's) that accounts for the fragmentation of the curriculum that is reported by Powell, Farrar, and Cohen. That
formalistic theory, according to Hirsch, has allowed administrators to remain "scrupulously neutral with regard to content."[35] Hirsch misses the point. If there is any
explanation for the chaos in the curriculum and the disengagement on the part of
students that *Shopping Mall* explores (taking that book to be a reasonably accurate depiction of what goes on in American secondary schools), it is the *absence*
of theory. The picture that Powell, Farrar, and Cohen paint is one in which at least
some administrators and teachers accede to the demands of almost any interest
group with something to say about the curriculum. The central metaphor of the
shopping mall is meant to convey not a theoretical justification (formalistic or
otherwise) for school practice, but a series of shops where students may purchase
their educational wares more or less at random, some shoddy, some of high quality, and much that is in between. Anything goes.

    Rather than adherence to a formalistic theory, there is a largely unacknowl-
edged but deeply ingrained posture of *neutrality* on educational issues. If there
is a policy that guides the curriculum described in *Shopping Mall*, it is a policy
of no policy, or, more correctly, an admixture of everything that could be called
policy. "Secondary educators," the authors of *Shopping Mall* say, "have tried
to solve the problem of competing purposes by accepting all of them. . . ."[36] It
is true that this state of anarchy has permitted the powers that be to not insist
that what Hirsch calls "traditional literate materials"[37] be taught to all students,
but it surely is not because school boards, administrators, and teachers have
collectively subscribed to a theory (Rousseau's, Dewey's, or anyone else's) that
justifies such a practice. It is because American education is the product of a
potpourri of ideas interacting with significant social trends, and, taken together,
the schools' most comfortable posture is to teach almost anything. What we have
left, therefore, is a situation in which information of the sort that is embodied in

Hirsch's list actually may not be taught to a certain segment of the school population, usually America's underclass, but it is for reasons that are more political
than theoretical. Regrettably, Hirsch has chosen the expedient but misleading
route of identifying a putative bête noire in American education rather than
undertaking a serious analysis that might serve to explain why the conventional
curriculum Hirsch wants desperately to maintain seems to fail in the context of
modern American schooling.

A PRESCRIPTION FOR MEDIOCRITY—OR WORSE

In contrast to the picture of neutrality that is convincingly conveyed in *Shopping
Mall*, Hirsch poses his own dictum: "Educational policy always involves choices
between degrees of worthiness," a proposition that is true enough. But what is it
about the information embodied in Hirsch's list (or, for that matter, an anticipated
enlarged version of it) that makes it a wiser choice than coming truly to understand a few things like Newtonian physics or the plays of Sophocles? Why is
naming lots of things so central to what Hirsch defines as a good education?
Hirsch's answer is that cultural literacy as an educational policy "helps us make
decisions because it places a higher value on national rather than local information."[38] Virginians, therefore, should choose to study Abraham Lincoln rather than
Jeb Stuart because Lincoln is part of our national language and Stuart is not.
Worthiness, it would seem, consists of two interrelated elements: The first is uni-
versality of vocabulary, at least extending to national boundaries; and the second
is (and here I must resort to the vernacular) to talk a good game. Hirsch would
have us believe, therefore, that the decisions of the Supreme Court are intrinsi-
cally more important for us to know than the shenanigans that take place at the
local courthouse, and that, of all the forms of knowledge to which one can aspire,
fragmented word-and-phrase recognition is the indispensable prerequisite. We are
being asked to give the highest priority in educational policy to the advancement
of "a universally shared national vocabulary."[39] Once we master that vocabulary,
we can pretend that we are educated. Hirsch has compared his own goal of cultural literacy with that of Professor Henry Higgins in Shaw's *Pygmalion*.[40] The
analogy is an apt one. Shaw sought to demonstrate that social-class distinctions—
the difference between a duchess and a Covent-Garden flower girl—were shal-
low and superficial, and after a short cram course, Eliza Doolittle was taught to
talk a good game and successfully passed for a duchess. The real question, however, is whether becoming educated is analogous to learning the mechanics of
diction that is standard in upper-crust English society. A superficial knowledge
of the vocabulary of educated people is hardly a substitute for becoming truly
educated. Shaw never implied, even remotely, that Eliza was being truly educated.
Quite the reverse. He was demonstrating that adopting the superficial trappings

of Britain's upper class could fool the world. A serious educational reform, presumably, does not set out to fool anyone but to educate successfully. Perhaps Hirsch's ideal of a "universally shared national vocabulary" cannot exactly be described as *unworthy*, but intellectual mastery of one's life situation, a fundamental comprehension of the disciplines of knowledge, a genuine appreciation for the arts, including a sensitivity to beauty, and coming to a workable understanding of the social and political realities of one's own society and the modern world surely are nobler educational ideals than a shared national vocabulary, which is analogous, in Hirsch's own words, "to a universal currency like the dollar."[41] If degree of worthiness is really the issue, as Hirsch claims, then his own priorities need serious re-examination.

Hirsch would have us believe that schoolchildren, who "are fascinated by straightforward information and absorb it without strain,"[42] can simply master his vocabulary list or a forthcoming expansion of it as a prerequisite to coming to a real understanding of what their culture represents. Let's be serious, Professor Hirsch! Aladdin and the Wonderful Lamp and the Wizard of Oz (two of the items on your list) may pass such muster, but have you really considered such items as amortization, anal personality, *deus ex machina*, and vestal virgin? I have known children whose absorption in such matters as prehistoric life has led them to amazing feats of memory when it comes to naming the varieties of dinosaurs that once existed on this planet, but Hirsch's alphabetical list has no such boundaries, and his claim as to the limits of children's capacities (or perhaps willingness) to define thousands of terms unrelated to their interests simply defies ordinary common sense and human experience. The implicit or explicit promise that memorizing these vocabulary items will stand children in good stead at some remote time in the future simply does not have the motivating power to overcome the sheer tedium that such an effort requires. And if Hirsch imagines that all those thousands of items can be framed in convenient cognitive frameworks that will ensure their retention, then he has forgotten the realities of school life. It is Hirsch, in the end, who is the hopeless romantic, not Rousseau or Dewey.

Hirsch's psychological justification for his proposal does in fact allude to what he calls "the psychological structure of background knowledge," and he cites a number of fascinating studies indicating, for example, that the prototypes that become part of our cognitive apparatus and sometimes are called frames, concepts, or models provide the basis for our ability to store knowledge in a retrievable form and to organize knowledge generally. These studies relating to what Hirsch calls schemata, he concludes, raise the question as to which ones, and in what circumstances, can be introduced into the education of children as a basis for equipping them with the cognitive structures they need. Admittedly, I may be missing Hirsch's point, but it seems to me that the clear implication of the series of psychological studies that he cites is that early education should concentrate on what he calls "primary associations"[43] that in the long run may lead to an extensive knowledge of specifics. Hirsch uses these studies as an argument for his contention that "the shared schemata necessary for reading and writing are always those of the wider community," but this is only in a very narrow geographical sense (an emphasis, for example, on a national rather than regional vocabulary). The far more significant upshot of the studies that Hirsch cites so approvingly is that those central concepts, ideas, and schemata may indeed become the avenue for furthering a richer and more functional conceptual apparatus, one that offers some promise of helping children master the intellectual constructs and modes of thought that are at the heart of academic culture. But that educational ideal is a far cry from the list of 5,000 or so informational items whose only organizational structure is alphabetical order.

Hirsch has every right to be concerned about the state of American education, especially the extent to which the finest elements of academic culture are being successfully taught. He raises intriguing questions about developing cognitive structures that are consistent with the research that he cites, but he chooses instead to make his list of disconnected and fragmented terms and phrases the centerpiece of his proposal. His leanings in terms of cognitive psychology notwithstanding, his obvious choice in the end is to emphasize encyclopedic mastery of information. He has the audacity to defend the inane educational pronouncements of Mr. Gradgrind in *Hard Times* as an "old prejudice"[44] on the ground that storing young minds with facts is reprehensible only when the facts are not interconnected, which is true enough, but how the thousands of items on Hirsch's list represent any sort of coherence is left only to one's imagination. Beyond the bald claim that they represent a national vocabulary and that appropriate schemata hold out some promise for more effective retention of information, those terms have about as much coherence as the Boston telephone directory. Hirsch does not advocate, for example, that all students actually study *Romeo and Juliet* (which on Hirsch's cultural literacy list follows *Roman numerals: I, V, X, L, C, D, M, romanticism*, and *Rome*). He requires only that "students have *some* information about *Romeo and Juliet*."[45] Presumably, knowing that it is a play by Shakespeare, that it is a story of two lovers, or that it ends tragically, is sufficient. It may indeed be true that knowing those things about Shakespeare's play is better than knowing nothing at all. It may even be remotely possible that even those bits of information can command entry into a world beyond superficial information. But, if that is the case, where are the interconnections that Hirsch claims makes these facts worth remembering, and how exactly do they provide entry into the world that lies beyond mere information? Hirsch, for all his commitment to the virtues of encyclopedic knowledge, is forced to admit in the end that "[t]o understand how isolated facts fit together in some coherent way, we must always acquire mental models of how they cohere, and these schemata can come only from detailed intensive study and experience."[46] True enough, but if that is Hirsch's honest conviction, then the focus of his book should have been on those mental models and how they could be incorporated into the curriculum rather than on "what every American needs to know" in such excruciating detail.

In fairness to Hirsch, he does not propose that what he calls the extensive curriculum (essentially, cultural literacy) constitutes the entire curriculum. He explicitly leaves room for what he calls the intensive curriculum, whose purpose is to encourage "a fully developed understanding of a subject [and] making one's knowledge of it integrated and coherent."[47] But, as Hirsch himself declares, "The consciously conveyed extensive curriculum is the new part of my proposal."[48] In the real world of schools, however, it is precisely the extensive curriculum that predominates and the intensive curriculum that is massively neglected. Teachers are already attempting (with understandable resistance on the part of students) to cram names, dates, and places into their heads. Hirsch's call for cultural literacy as the goal of American schooling and his emphasis on cultural literacy with highly specific factual information as its hallmark easily could become the modern equivalent of faculty psychology. When teachers in the nineteenth century concentrated their teaching around meaningless drills, rote memorization, and useless exercises, they could always claim that these activities had the virtue of strengthening mental faculties such as memory and will. Now, Hirsch has provided modern-day teachers with a justification for inflicting the same tasks on children under the banner of cultural literacy.

For years, it has been known that the standard pattern of classroom discourse is the question and answer and that the predominant emphasis in terms of the subject matter of classroom language is factual information. Although the evidence as to what actually is taught in schools is anything but complete, studies of classroom behavior—from Romiett Stevens's 1912 study of questioning in the classroom,[49] to *The Language of the Classroom* more than a half century later,[50] and extending through a substantial review of research in that area by James Hoetker and William Ahlbrand—have attested to the persistence of the question-and-answer format in classroom practice, with factual questioning predominating. Hoetker and Ahlbrand, for example, reported that as late as 1950, "the recitation of textbook facts was still the 'representative' method of teaching in American schools," and that studies through the late 1960s "show a remarkable stability of classroom patterns of verbal behavior over the last half century."[51] In a more recent study of classroom behavior, Susan Stodolsky, Teresa Ferguson, and Karen Wimpelberg noted that although the recitation as a form of classroom discourse occurs more frequently in mathematics classes than in social studies,[52] even in social studies, "the dominant goal is receiving information (62%), followed by about one-fourth of the segments oriented toward learning concepts and skills."[53] Finally, drawing on a study involving observational data from over 1,000 elementary and secondary schools, Kenneth Sirotkin concluded that "the modal classroom patterns consist of (1) the teacher explaining or lecturing to the total class or to a single student, asking direct, factual questions, or monitoring students; and (2) the students ostensibly listening to the teacher or responding to teacher-initiated interaction."[54] By contrast, the likelihood of students participating in other activities, such as discussion, simulation, role playing, and demonstration is less than 8 percent.[55] The practices rarely observed in the study are precisely ones that are associated with "formalistic theory," such as questioning at higher cognitive levels and student decision making.[56] Rather than the specter of formalistic theory driving day-to-day classroom practice, the recitation as form and factual information as content have remained for many years the most familiar features of classroom life. Hirsch's remedy for ailing American schools is to do more of the same.

PROBABLE CONSEQUENCES

The alienation of students from school knowledge is a real problem, not a phoney one. The result is that many students are denied the opportunity to enter into the world beyond commonsense realities, which disciplined knowledge offers. In response to that problem, however, Hirsch has conjured up a demon of classroom life (formalistic theory), which is the source of the deficiencies that he finds in modern American schooling, and, not surprisingly, his remedies consist largely of what is happening already. Even worse, he has extracted his names, dates, places, and expressions from the context of the disciplines in which they are found and has organized them into a stock list. The most likely result of presenting students with such a list to master is not so much open rebellion as a quiet resistance consisting of setting forth the correct answers (as far as possible) in return for grades or credentials and then disassociating themselves from what the scraps of information are supposed to represent. Hirsch himself concludes that "the very existence of a list will cause students merely to memorize the bare items it contains and learn nothing significant at all. Students will trivialize cultural information without really possessing it." With remarkable candor, he goes on to admit, "How can I deny that such misuse of the list is not only a danger but a near certainty?"[57] As if to ensure that dangerous course, Hirsch suggests the possibility of developing general knowledge tests for three different stages of schooling, each based upon an agreed-on body of information."[58] If those educational practices are really the probable consequences of Hirsch's proposal, and the reduction of academic culture to a trivia game does indeed become even more widespread than it is already, then he may have a lot to answer for.

"Coverage" is already one of the most familiar facets of classroom life. One of Hirsch's most important misconceptions is that the lack of knowledge he finds among students is attributable to a lack of effort on the part of teachers to provide the kind of information on his list. The real question is not why don't American schools emphasize the acquisition of information; the question is why do so many students systematically reject it. In one highly perceptive analysis of the realities of American schooling, Linda McNeil argues that "[t]he simplest and most notorious lecture technique among social studies teachers is the reduction of any topic to fragments or disjointed pieces of information—lists. A list lets a teacher avoid having to elaborate or show linkages, and it keeps students, especially those weak at reading and writing, from having to express 'learnings' in complete sentences and paragraphs. No one is called upon to synthesize or give a picture of interrelationships."[59] Can there be any doubt that the appearance of tests of cultural literacy will serve only to accelerate that fragmentation of knowledge? The contemporary disengagement of students from the knowledge that schools have to offer will not be helped merely by intensifying our insistence that students learn it. It can be helped if both the form and content of classroom instruction are transformed to the point where students are able to perceive the relationship between school knowledge and their own empowerment. Poor Dewey conceived of an education where knowledge could be reintegrated into the context of human experience, but the structure and function of classroom life have remained relatively unchanged, and now we face massive alienation on the part of not only students but even some teachers. At its core, Hirsch's solution is simply to insist that teachers teach and students learn the kinds informational items that make up his list. Lacking the delicacy of the fabled curate, I am forced to conclude that while certain parts of the egg that Hirsch has cooked up may be excellent, as a whole it smells really bad.

CHAPTER 8

One Kind of Excellence:
Ensuring Academic Achievement
at La Salle High School

CO-AUTHORED WITH CALVIN R. STONE

How is a good school structured and sustained? There are undoubtedly several approaches to such a question, but one way of getting at the answer is by actually examining a school that is by some common standard an excellent school. La Salle High School (a fictional name but not a fictional school) was chosen for study because the graduates of that high school well exceeded expectations as to academic success in their freshman year of college. Considering the relatively high socioeconomic status of La Salle's population, its graduates were predicted to do well in college, but they did even better than graduates of other schools similarly situated. There are undoubtedly other criteria of excellence that could be asserted and defended, but graduates' success as college students can hardly be dismissed.

At a certain level, present-day advocates of educational reform agree that a rigorous curriculum accompanied by high standards should be part of what we mean by an excellent school. What often is overlooked when such demands are made, however, is the nature of the structures that are necessary in order to maintain such a level of excellence. Simply asserting them or even requiring them by imposing dire penalties does not in itself ensure success. La Salle High School did not simply stipulate academic excellence as a standard; it instituted procedures and structures that were aimed at providing the support that such high expectations required. No school is a perfect school, but the way in which La Salle High School was organized provides one way to approach the problem of providing academic excellence for all.

Nobody is against excellent schools. While there is, for all intents and purposes, no disagreement on that subject, an unresolved question remains as to what in the world we mean by excellence. There is a long history in educational research of trying to identify with scientific precision the commonly held characteristics of good teachers, good administrators, and good schools, but these efforts are now falling into disrepute (or at least ought to be). Instead, what seems to be emerging is the more plausible idea that there are many kinds of excellence in these matters and, therefore, a variety of schools regarded as excellent may not share precisely the same characteristics.

Even when we narrow the field to one type of educational institution, say, the high school, and even when we concentrate on one facet of excellence, say, academic excellence, excellent schools appear to differ about as much from one another as they do from poor schools as a group. Excellent academic high schools, for example, may not even share what are regarded as highly significant structural characteristics, such as whether or not tracking is practiced. Even when there is tracking across two high schools and even when they are in the same school district, there is good evidence to indicate that the practices may manifest themselves in widely disparate ways.[1] Much seems to depend on how institutional cultures affect the behavior of key actors and what countervailing forces exist to mitigate undesirable outcomes that may be associated with those structural features of schooling.

One other aspect of excellent schools often is overlooked. No school is uniformly excellent. Whatever the genuine excellence exhibited by a given school, whatever favorable reputation it may enjoy, whatever have been its awards and accolades, it is still possible to discover negative features. In many cases, these negative features are in the nature of trade-offs. In other words, in order to achieve one form of excellence, a school may define itself in a certain way (officially or not), and implementing that kind of excellence may, here and there, impede the achievement of excellence in another respect. One avenue for addressing this state of affairs is to try to identify schools that are widely accepted as excellent in one respect or another, and then, by immersing oneself in the culture of that school, seek to delineate what that school's excellence consists of as well as what trade-offs may have been made in order to achieve it. La Salle High School was selected for such a study because an examination of the records of its graduates indicated an unusually high degree of academic success as college freshmen, even when factors such as socioeconomic status were controlled. While academic success in college as a measure of the excellence of high schools sometimes is disparaged in educational circles, preparation for college reflects a significant and abiding function of American high schools. To be sure, one can identify other kinds of excellence, but it seems reasonable to assume that if graduates of a particular high school enjoy unexpectedly high academic success in college, then there must be something in the way academic subjects were treated in the high school they attended that could account for that success.

THE COMMUNITY SERVED BY LA SALLE HIGH SCHOOL

La Salle High School serves no single community and, in fact, its physical location does not place it readily within a community context. The school grounds lie within a residential area of fine homes located near a major highway. There is no business district adjacent to the school nor are there any of the sandwich shops and ice cream parlors that tend to grow up around large high schools. This physical arrangement may be significant in that the area immediately surrounding La Salle provides no convenient haven for school resisters who wish to escape the school environs for a couple of hours or for the full day.

The school serves about 2,000 students drawn primarily from four separate residential communities that tend to range from middle class to upper middle class. Students in general feel that this residential community identification remains reasonably strong during the high school years, and to some extent it forms the basis for the cliques that are part of every high school setting. The identification with four communities rather than one also may account for the fact that La Salle athletic events tend to draw small crowds, as do other social events, such as school dances. It may be that because the primary community identification tends to remain localized, La Salle High School, in effect, is perceived by students and school personnel alike as a place where adolescents from four communities come to be educated. While the school might function to a limited extent as a center of social and recreational activities for adolescents, we found almost no perception by students or adults that the school is actually a focal point for social life or community solidarity. Although teachers and administrators sometimes express concern over this aspect of their school, the situation tends to reinforce their notions that school is strictly a place to get an education—in this case, a rigorously academic one.

Approximately 80 to 85% of La Salle graduates obtain further education at the college level, and an additional 5% go on to trade schools. In part at least, these are reflections of the value that the community places on academics. Other indicators are that 72% of the heads of families in the La Salle district have attended college, and about 25% of the heads of families of La Salle students have postgraduate degrees. Using the Duncan Socioeconomic Index as a scale of reference, the mean for heads of families of La Salle students is 57.5, which is high, but not as high as other high schools that were under consideration for this study. Compared with one other high school, for example, a greater percentage of the parents of La Salle students tend to work in business than in the professions, such as law and medicine. The key reason for choosing La Salle was that, even with that profile, La Salle graduates tended to enjoy more success as college freshmen than was predicted. While high-socioeconomic status is statistically associated with academic success, it is certainly no guarantee.

Two of the four communities that La Salle High School serves are reputed to have a large Jewish population, and it is likely that the school has the highest population of Jewish students in this midwestern state. Teachers and administrators seem particularly conscious of this ethnic cast to the school and associate it with the school's pronounced commitment to academic excellence. Estimates of the Jewish population in La Salle by school personnel ranged from about 30% to as high as 75%. Although no definitive figures exist, our own estimates indicated that the actual percentage is between 20 and 25%. What is significant, however, is not the actual figure but the perception on the part of administrators and teachers that there is indeed a large population of Jewish parents who bring with them their traditional press for academic achievement.

This perception of a press for academic achievement from the community, whether it comes specifically from Jewish parents or, as is more likely, from a value shared by the predominantly non-Jewish middle-class parents, is an ever-present reality to the teachers and administrators. Although educators at La Salle sometimes complain of having parents "on their back all the time," they also seem to derive from this situation a sense of legitimacy for the way they themselves define their professional roles, and this may account for some of the clearly exaggerated estimates of the Jewish population on the part of some school personnel. A large majority of the teachers and administrators see their roles as tied directly and almost exclusively to academic achievement, and the fact that the communities they serve seem to share that perception provides them with a mandate to pursue that mission with even greater dedication. At La Salle, there appears to be a close match between community expectations (perceived or actual) and professional role definition.

Some minority students reside in the four communities that La Salle High School serves, and this group is supplemented by approximately 120 Black students who are transported to the school from a nearby metropolitan area under Chapter 220, a federal program that permits parents from inner-city areas to enroll their children in nearby suburban schools. With respect to the Chapter 220 students, as they are called, it is likely that a parallel attitude toward school achievement to the one in the indigenous communities is functioning in the Black subgroup. Approximately 50% of the Chapter 220 students come to La Salle from parochial schools, indicating some history of parental concern for the education of their children. The combination of indigenous minority students and Chapter 220 students brings the total minority students at La Salle to 8 to 10%.

With respect to the Chapter 220 students, there is some evidence that special care has been taken to initiate them into the prevailing culture of La Salle High School. Teachers, administrators, and counselors report that these students have been forewarned of the rigorous academic standards in the school, and the students' progress is carefully monitored. The time of our study coincided with the first year in which Chapter 220 students were being graduated, and, although no actual figures existed at the time, school counselors reported that a high percentage of these students were making plans for college. A special minority counselor had been hired, presumably to deal with problems that might arise with respect to the minority population in the school.

Although the Chapter 220 students seem genuinely welcome at La Salle, there is also a special determination on the part of the professional staff to see to it that the character of the school, with its overwhelming emphasis on high academic achievement, will not be altered by this population. At one school board meeting, the superintendent made a point of reassuring the members of the board that the Chapter 220 students were indeed measuring up to La Salle's high academic standards and that there was no indication that those standards were being lowered in any way.

ORGANIZATIONAL CHARACTERISTICS OF LA SALLE HIGH SCHOOL

The La Salle High School building is also the site for the offices of the district administration. The school superintendent, Dr. Hallquist, has his office in the high school, and his physical presence in the building makes him not only the chief executive officer in the district, but, in effect, the chief administrator of the school. Unlike many school superintendents in larger districts, he is intimately involved in the instructional activities of the school and, in fact, during the year of this study, acceded to the school board's request that he personally visit each teacher's classroom for the purpose of evaluating instruction. Needless to say, the actual presence of a school superintendent in a classroom for purposes of teacher evaluation is a rarity in an age where the bureaucratization of schooling has served to define the role of superintendent essentially in terms of budget matters, school politics, and public relations.

Also contrary to the popular image of school superintendents as ex-football coaches is Dr. Hallquist's status as an ex-Latin teacher and his reputation as an intellectual. One school administrator in another part of the state acknowledged that, in contrast to Dr. Hallquist, he does not have the "brains" to deal with the kind of community that La Salle serves nor could he deal successfully with such a high-powered school board. In one of our first visits with Dr. Hallquist, he showed us a five-page memorandum he had drafted and distributed to the faculty outlining his reaction to a new book critical of modern education. In general, he expressed approval of the book's negative stance toward certain modern educational trends and supported the book's more or less conservative educational philosophy. Whatever his leanings in terms of educational ideologies, however, it is clear that Dr. Hallquist reads books, even books on pedagogy!

Dr. Hallquist's presence in La Salle High School is supplemented by the presence of school personnel who in other circumstances would be housed away from the scene of the action in remote administrative offices off the school grounds. In larger school districts, key administrative and support personnel frequently are physically detached from the day-to-day reality of school life. At La Salle, however, Mr. Brown, to take one example, the hard-working and widely respected curriculum coordinator, also has his office in the building and works in daily contact with high school teachers and administrators. Mr. Brown also presides over the powerful Administrative Council comprising the department heads of the various subject departments as well as the chief librarian. Consistent with the overwhelmingly academic emphasis at La Salle High School, it is the department heads with their traditional commitment to their academic specializations who wield considerable power in the school. It is the department head, for example, who is entrusted with the main responsibility for teacher evaluation, a responsibility that takes on even greater significance in a school district where seniority is only one of several factors considered and where teacher competence ratings play a major role. (Apparently, at some point during contract negotiations, the teachers' union made this concession in return for certain benefits.) These teacher evaluations, which usually take place at least two, but sometimes as many as five, times a year generally are conducted by teams of two persons, the department head plus one other member of the administrative staff. This system provides some degree of protection against the possibility that a rating might be unfair or dictated by personal animosity.

These structural characteristics at La Salle appear to be quite distinctive in the state. In other high schools under study, department heads have lower status; they are primarily teachers, not administrators, and do not bear major responsibility for evaluating the other teachers in their departments. By contrast, at least some other high schools turn that function over almost exclusively to the principal and assistant principals, who often, by their own admission, either express inadequacy to the task or maintain that they do not have sufficient time to evaluate teachers effectively. Furthermore, the department heads at La Salle tend to be regarded as scholars who bring to their considerable administrative responsibilities a distinctively academic bias. In fact, our interviews with department heads indicate that, as a group, they pride themselves not only on their teaching ability, but on their standing as scholars and intellectuals, a self-perception that probably is warranted.

Sharing the usual administrative responsibilities at La Salle High School are two co-principals. They divide the duties for student disciplinary problems, truancy, and the day-to-day management of the school. This shared principalship tends to diffuse the overall authority of each, thus ensuring that Dr. Hallquist remains the overall administrator in charge. Quite a few students, for example, believe that Dr. Hallquist is the school principal rather than the chief district administrator, an understandable confusion when he is present and observable on a daily basis in the high school.

There are also some rather unusual features to the counseling situation at La Salle. Perhaps most obvious is that the ratio of counselors to students runs somewhere between 1:200 and 1:250, as compared with some secondary schools in the state where the ratio was as high as 1:400 at the time of the study. Second, counselors are relieved of almost all responsibility for administrative duties, such as scheduling of students. While many counselors in other schools find their roles defined as quasi-administrators, the counselors at La Salle devote by far the major portion of their professional work to direct contact with students. Their calendars are filled with appointments for counseling sessions that relate to academic matters, college or vocational planning, and personal problems. Undoubtedly, this favorable situation results at least in part from the fact that a considerable share of administrative responsibility is undertaken by the department heads, such as the placement of students in different level classes. Decisions such as the dropping of classes by students, for example, are primarily the province of department heads, not counselors.

PUBLIC ACCOUNTABILITY VERSUS PROFESSIONAL AUTONOMY

As already indicated, the geographic communities served by La Salle High School are inhabited primarily by middle- and upper-middle-class families. Educators in the La Salle district who were interviewed, without exception, perceived the community as a whole and the parents of La Salle students in particular as having extremely high expectations of the school. These community expectations arc perceived to be focused directly on the academic program of the high school and on the development of students' potential for success in future university work. This perception of a "push" by the community for academic excellence was made all the more stark when seen against the educators' perceptions that the community has only a passing interest in the success of the school's athletic program or social activities.

This community press for academic excellence is felt by educators through direct contact with parents, who are perceived to be extremely involved and quite demanding. It also is reflected in the actions of the school board, which is perceived by the school staff as being dominated by individuals who are highly intelligent, businesslike, self-confident, aggressive in their desire to involve themselves with educational issues, and firm and decisive in setting a course for the school. The activities of the school board are not limited to concern for the development of the successful student at La Salle. Indeed, in the year prior to this study, the school board had requested that administrators produce documentation for each student who had dropped out, including a description of the problems that the student encountered and the actions taken by the school to resolve them. Needless to say, this request in itself caused school personnel to reconsider problems faced by marginal students and ways that the school might respond.

Although some complaints are voiced, the staff of the school actually appears to take some pride in the fact that the school board is as powerful and decisive as it is, because this enhances La Salle's reputation for excellence. There are, however, reservations expressed about the role that the school board plays. One teacher remarked that she wished that the board would leave more educational decisions in the hands of professional educators. A second teacher, who represents a more critical extreme, stated, "The [school] board is made up of captains of industry, and they seem to think they can treat us [teachers] like the clerks in their stores or the laborers on their assembly lines." This critical perception by teachers of the school board's power is voiced by other educators as well, but most often is focused on one particular issue that stands as a source of friction between the school board and the teachers: that teachers in the district may be laid off using criteria other than seniority. In a period of declining enrollments, several teachers each year, regardless of their time in service to the district, were being laid off. The district's legal authority to use criteria other than seniority, such as teaching competence, places the district in a commanding position to demand excellence from its teaching staff, but that obviously has its costs.

Leaving aside the implications of the relationship between the school board and the teachers, we at least can conclude that there is a strong consensus among La Salle educators that the community places an extremely high value on education and that parents support the school by demanding excellence, not only of their sons and daughters, but also of educators. In addition, these values and expectations are reflected in the community's electing school board officials who are vocal and aggressive in their demand for academic excellence. As already indicated, however, academic excellence is a frequently expressed goal of American high schools. As such, it has become a kind of slogan that is in such general use that it has little power to explain a school's success unless it is defined further by attention to the concrete school practices that are derived from the meaning that "academic excellence" has for educators. One of the obvious costs of this kind of excellence, which may be particular to this case, is the strong tilt at La Salle High School away from professional autonomy and toward public accountability. Teacher morale, for example, became a particular factor when nine teachers and one guidance counselor were laid off (a couple were later rehired) during the year of this study. In the absence of firm job security, it was natural for teachers to ask themselves who would be cast adrift the following year. In an attempt to mitigate the problem of laid-off teachers, Dr. Hallquist secured the school board's permission to hire, at a cost to the board of $500 per teacher, an occupational counseling firm to assist the laid-off teachers in making career changes. Overall, however, La Salle High School generally was regarded by its professional staff as a good place to be, even though many teachers and counselors remained understandably anxious about job security.

Notwithstanding the real concern that teachers express about job security, it is still safe to say that the ethos of La Salle High School is one of strict professionalism, including a strong sense of duty and accountability both to the students and to the community. While every teachers' lounge has its share of banter and idle chatter, it is distinctly less pronounced at La Salle than at other high schools that were observed. By and large, teachers prepare for classes, correct papers, and attend to record keeping. In one instance, a foreign language teacher was asked what work she was engaged in so busily in the teachers' lounge. It turned out that she had received a higher than expected estimate from a travel agency for a forthcoming trip to Europe with her students. She was using her free period to write directly to hostels and bus companies in Europe to see whether she could reduce the cost of the trip by making the travel arrangements herself. This represents a degree of dedication and commitment that is expected of and not uncommon among La Salle teachers.

Given the fact that most La Salle teachers are evaluated between two and five times a year, and that La Salle teachers' continued employment depends at least to some extent on meeting the standards that are defined by the evaluation process, it is clear that La Salle's teachers are subject to tremendous "pressure from the top" to excel in the roles defined by and for them. In this regard, it is important to note that the teachers at La Salle are, in a sense, held accountable for the actions of their students. Teachers who were interviewed, for example, were conscious of the fact that their success in the evaluation process depended on the extent to which students appeared to be motivated, asked questions, and assumed responsibility in the classroom setting.

It is inconceivable that a teacher observed at a nearby high school, who failed over 48% of his students, could define his role in the same way were he teaching at La Salle. First, he would not be meeting many of the standards and expectations upon which La Salle teachers are judged. Second, at La Salle High School, there is such a self-conscious regard for community expectations that, in such a case, this teacher's particular practices and perhaps his overall competence would become immediately suspect. Whether or not it is actually the case, there is a perceived expectation on the part of school personnel that La Salle parents would become aggressively involved in demanding changes in the event of such an occurrence, and there is little doubt as well that their efforts would be reasonably successful. And finally, at La Salle not only are individual teachers rigorously evaluated, but so is the curriculum. If, at La Salle, a course taught by several teachers was discovered to have a high failure rate, the course itself would come under scrutiny as well as the practices of the individual teachers.

While interviews of educators at La Salle indicate that an actual case of this nature (a teacher failing an extremely high proportion of students) has not occurred, one revealing incident may serve to illustrate the institutional ethos at La Salle. Some of the details of the incident probably have been changed or recast in the telling, but, in general, the story is as follows: A La Salle teacher gave a student a B for a semester grade. The student and parents of the student objected, arguing that the student should have received an A. The teacher refused to change the grade, and so, under pressure from the parents, several administrators conducted a hearing. The student's grade hinged on the fact that the teacher had given the student a B in on important composition, and the student and his parents argued that the student deserved an A for the composition. To resolve the stalemate that ensued, school officials suggested that the composition be sent to a national testing service for evaluation and that both teacher and student agree to abide by the judgment. The composition received an A, and the student's grade was subsequently changed. Although this incident is an isolated one, it was repeated by several informants and has become part of the folklore of La Salle High School. Teachers and administrators feel themselves to be under the watchful eye of aggressive, articulate parents, and this strongly influences their professional behavior.

The incident also serves to illustrate several important aspects of La Salle's approach to accountability. First, teachers have relatively limited autonomy and are certainly not "autocrats of the classroom," a term that was applied to teachers at another high school. At La Salle, teachers are respected for their teaching ability and for their mastery of subject matter, but they must exercise caution in their dealings with students lest they be called to account. Second, the incident illustrates the aggressive role that parents of La Salle students take or at least are believed to take. Their own high level of educational attainment and perhaps their social standing confer on them a certain freedom to challenge teachers' decisions. In addition, the solution to the problem (using an independent evaluator to grade the student's composition) indicates how far school authorities will go to accommodate parental concern for high academic standing. Finally, this and similar incidents reflect and illustrate the contours of the relationship that exists between individual educators and the communities La Salle serves.

FORMAL AND INFORMAL STRUCTURES OF AUTHORITY AT LA SALLE

As already indicated, a prominent feature of La Salle's day-to-day reality is the community mandate to strive for and to achieve academic excellence. This mandate and its ramifications permeate the school's approach to maintaining authority because the classes that a student takes and the amount of freedom that students have during the school day when they are not in formal classes is largely determined by their academic performance. In fact, La Salle may be seen as having built its institutional life around the legitimacy of academic excellence, but, practically speaking, in order for that definition of excellence to be maintained, mechanisms had to be created to ensure that all or almost all of the school's students would be able to find success as the school's staff and community define it. A low rate of student success would undermine the legitimacy of the school's authority. Therefore, it is highly significant that the formal authority structure in the school is undergirded by an informal authority structure, which serves those students who otherwise might have difficulty in meeting the school's academic standards. Thus, academic success as a definition of excellence survives only when it actually can be achieved, and the authority structures of the school, formal and informal, must be marshalled to achieve it.

The heart of La Salle's formal structure is an emphasis on careful diagnosis of academic problems, an extensive system of support for students encountering academic difficulty, and an especially close monitoring of student progress. A rather complex network of support for a defined standard of excellence keeps the system working and prevents a great many students from "falling through the cracks," as one administrator put it. The formal structure includes the following:

1. Students are tested upon entry into the district to determine their levels of academic skills. These tests include "both cognitive abilities and a writing sample which indicates writing skills." Students then are tentatively placed in classes for the purpose of further diagnosis. This tentative placement allows La Salle's professional staff to evaluate further student capabilities by observing their actual levels of performance.
2. Students then are assigned by subject to one of four academic levels, Honors, A, B, and C. Level B is the most common placement and incorporates about 50% of the student population. In some cases, students may be placed in a high academic track for several subjects but a lower academic track in other academic areas according to their performance. The administrators interviewed stressed the idea that placement is "based on performance rather than ability." They stated that the criteria used for placement include: (a) achievement testing; (b) motivation as perceived by the classroom teacher; and (c) the grades that students are receiving. Each academic department, primarily through the department head, does its own placement, and there is a re-sorting at the end of each semester based on the student's semester performance. Parents, however, may intervene in this process by requesting either a higher or lower placement for students and, most often, parent requests are granted "with a note inserted in the student record indicating that the placement is not the recommendation of the department."
3. The La Salle staff periodically tests student development and retention; for example, at one point, a mathematics test given to juniors indicated that approximately 25% of the school's juniors could not achieve an eighth-grade level of performance in arithmetic with 80% proficiency. Accordingly, those students were given remedial instruction. This incident led to the establishment of a school-wide mathematics maintenance program in order to ensure that students obtained and retained basic mathematics skills.
4. In their freshman year, all students are required to attend study halls during the hour or two when they are not in class. The study halls are also resource centers, which contain many of the books and references needed by freshmen

in their courses. In such study centers, emphasis is placed on assisting students with their work. The teacher aide who runs the center is familiar with the assignments that freshmen receive. (This stands in contrast to study halls in other schools, which provide only custodial care during study periods.) Some freshmen who are deemed to be academically deficient are required to attend a separate study skills center adjacent to the freshman study hall. There, the intention is to provide more intense help than is available in the freshman study hall. Together, the freshman study hall and the study skills center serve to initiate freshmen into the academic culture of the school.

5. During their sophomore, junior, and senior years students who are experiencing academic or truancy problems are assigned to study halls during times when they are not in class. Again, emphasis is on providing academic assistance.
6. A few students exhibiting extraordinary behavioral problems are assigned to "supervised study." In this room, custodial care is supplemented with a strong emphasis on interaction between the aide and the students. The room has only 12 desks, indicating that supervised study is necessary for only a tiny portion of the student population.
7. The school places a premium on student attendance in classes and has designed an effective monitoring system whereby parents are notified by the classroom teacher of class cuts on the same day that they take place.

In explaining the district's rationale for assigning freshmen to specific study areas during those portions of the day when they are not in formal classes, La Salle educators emphasize the various study areas' potential for providing specific forms of academic help to students. Each of the study areas also is seen as a means of providing an appropriate structure that facilitates keeping students on task. Study areas are staffed by aides and by professional staff who "have a knack for working with students" and who, as previously mentioned, are aware on a day-to-day basis of the various student assignments. None of these areas, including the most closely supervised study halls, is seen by administrators as punitive in nature, and each is designed to provide much more than custodial care.

Examination of the La Salle approach indicates that the formal network of support systems serves to ensure a high degree of academic success. In general outline, the network not only consists of diagnosis, monitoring, and evaluation, but also entails "training the student to receive help." It is in this respect that administrators express a belief that providing students opportunities for study in and of itself is insufficient, since many students will ignore those opportunities. Accordingly, further training is seen as necessary, and the burden of this "training" falls primarily on the aides and professional staff who manage the various study areas. The implication of the administrators is that through a nonthreatening but rigorously monitored relationship, focusing on individual academic development, the aides and staff members are able to encourage or cajole students in the direction of academic achievement. Thus, the aides as well as the teachers play a key role in diagnosis, supervision, and tutoring. Unlike at other high schools, the study hall period is integral to the school's overall program.

Our impression, relative to programs in other high schools being observed, is that at La Salle the mandate for academic excellence has become the medium through which the staff communicates with students. This is a distinctly different emphasis from that taken by programs that focus more directly on aspects of social development or on adolescent problems. The La Salle administrators perceive that the academic focus provides a more benign environment with respect to negative labeling than would a direct attack on students' problems in terms of emotional and social adjustment.

In some respects, the academic focus tends to mitigate negative labeling because it generally is restricted to dealing with specific student behaviors as opposed to identifying personal character traits; for example, there is a significant difference between, on one hand, telling a student that his or her absences are affecting the quality of schoolwork and, on the other, suggesting that those absences reflect a pattern of avoidance or are indicative of an emotional disorder. The relationship between absence and failure to achieve well academically can be seen by the student as temporary and subject to correction, while the labeling of the same behavior as abnormal suggests a serious and even permanent condition. In this way, the focus on academics may serve to avoid at least some potentially destructive labels. In general, the formal system of authority that prevails at La Salle is premised on encouraging students' attention to academic tasks and not on putative emotional disorders.

The formal structure of authority also prescribes general procedures aimed at groups of students. All students in their junior year, for example, take a test designed to measure general mathematics competence. Those students who do not pass this test at least at an 80% level of proficiency are required to take a mathematics refresher course. (This constitutes about 25% of the junior class.) Up to this point, this process may be perceived as simply an examination-driven approach to ensuring that La Salle students have achieved a prescribed level of competence. However, even after the mathematics refresher course, a few students still will not have demonstrated 80% proficiency on the skills tested, and it is for this small group that new mechanisms are set in motion. Rather than leaving these students to their own devices for developing mathematical competence, each of the students is further required to attend a mathematics laboratory at which individual problems with mathematics are diagnosed and treated on a case-by-case basis. These cases ranged from a simple lack of skill development to dealing with psychological phenomena such as reducing the effects of test anxiety and even developing means for teaching certain geometric functions to a blind student. (This meant producing teaching devices, as no commercial devices were available.)

In instances such as these, it is highly significant that, while the formal structure of authority imposes high expectations on all students, it also provides extensive support services and requires students to use those services. The proficiency requirement in mathematics would in itself be virtually meaningless unless a regular screening process existed to identify those students having difficulties and, more important, involved a carefully delineated procedure for correcting them. It is in this sense that La Salle's approach differs from the more common "standard raising" approach to achieving academic excellence. Frequently, schools, school districts, and state departments of education seek to achieve excellence simply by testing alone, by raising minimum requirements on such tests, or by simplistic mechanisms such as increasing graduation requirements. Because support systems for students are lacking or inadequate in some of these cases, excellence is not actually advanced, only proclaimed.

In spite of La Salle's general success in using academic development as a medium for maintaining authority in the school setting, the school goes to considerable lengths to deal with the problems presented by certain students who simply do not accept the school's authority structure as being legitimate. The major burden for dealing with problems of discipline and truancy falls on the two building co-principals, who are "the court of last resort" at La Salle. The principals report that in general their official approach is to take a hard line with both students and parents ("the student will have to shape up or get out") but, in practice, they tend to work behind the scenes to keep the students in school. The behind-the-scenes work may include intervention and student advocacy with the student's teachers and establishing contact with local employers to attempt to secure a job for a student. (The job can then become a part of the negotiation process—"If we got you an afternoon job, would you be willing to remain in school during the mornings?") It is also common for one of the two co-principals to send a student to the other when he or she feels unable to deal effectively with a particular case.

Thus, it appears that the formal and highly visible authority structure co-exists with a somewhat hidden and informal, but reasonably effective, informal authority structure. In other words, there is a human face behind some of the formal procedures.

DEFINING LA SALLE HIGH SCHOOL'S APPROACH
TO KNOWLEDGE AND TEACHING

With academic excellence as a mandate from the community and also as a central focus of the authority structure of the school, it follows that the school's educational responsibility would be similarly defined. In our very first interview with a La Salle teacher, we were told in unequivocal terms that "[t]his is a college-entrance school," and nothing in our subsequent experience there caused us to question that characterization. For the most part, the emphasis on academic achievement at La Salle, however, is not concentrated on mere mastery of specific facts and skills. Direct observation of classes at all levels indicates that, to a surprising extent, an interpretive and quite sophisticated approach to knowledge prevails in all four academic tracks.

In a U.S. history class, for example, students were presented with two competing hypotheses regarding the historical importance of the fact that a loose confederation of states existed in the decade prior to the ratification of the Constitution. In evaluating these hypotheses, the students were not presented with "correct" answers to the questions that arose but were required to interpret these events themselves. In this sense, students were "doing history" and were learning a process of interpretation that begins to approach the work of professional historians. This may be compared with the approach taken by some teachers at other schools under study where students often were asked to master the history that had already been interpreted by the authors of the textbook. Although both of these approaches to the study of history might be perceived as academic, they reflect quite different conceptions of what kind of knowledge is important. Some other schools' mode of instruction (textbook mastery) hardly ever extends beyond the immediate classroom situation, while La Salle's (inquiry and interpretation) may develop habits of thought that can be employed in a variety of circumstances.

In one chemistry class, the teacher presented a problem for the students to solve involving the number of grams of copper present in a solution of copper sulfate. One student, using calculus, presented his solution, which the teacher accepted. A second student presented her solution to the problem using algebra, which the teacher also accepted. Finally, using arithmetic, a third student presented still a third way of solving the problem. Each "correct" solution resulted in a slightly different answer. Clearly, this chemistry teacher was not presenting science problems as amenable to a single pre-specified procedure. There was no "right way" to solve the problem, and by conveying that, this chemistry teacher, consciously or subconsciously, was reflecting something of the excitement of engaging in scientific endeavor. In an Honors class, a widely respected English teacher elicited intricate and sophisticated interpretations of a short story by Willa Cather, to the obvious delight of a group of highly intelligent and motivated students. In a C track biology class, a "tough" science teacher challenged students to explain why the experiment, involving photosynthesis, that they had been conducting over the past several days did not turn out as expected.

In each of these cases, the emphasis on academic achievement was clearly evident; teachers were dealing directly with academic subject matter, not the broad needs and interests of students, but the conception of subject matter that was being represented was rich enough to convey at least something of the nature of scholarly inquiry. Had the emphasis on academics taken the form of mastering a few facts about the Articles of Confederation, finding *the* right solution to a sci-

in inquiry engages students

ence problem, merely reviewing the plot of a short story, or determining the right recipe for conducting a scientific experiment, it most likely would have served to alienate a large segment of the student population.

The school's curricular offerings, while predominantly reflecting a traditional subject-based framework, also incorporate a few courses that take a less traditional approach to subject matter. Students who are having personal and/or academic problems are directed to such courses by guidance counselors or by teachers who recognize the student's need for a more personal approach to subject matter through which teachers incorporate "extended role" responsibilities to students. Mr. Talbot, for example, is well known among the La Salle faculty as working very well with students who have school problems. During his earlier years as a member of La Salle's faculty, his definition of his professional role was quite typical of the La Salle teacher. Several years ago, however, in response to some student and parent requests, the high school began to offer courses in psychology. Mr. Talbot was chosen as one of the psychology teachers partly because of his academic interest in psychology and partly because his own self-explorations made him keenly aware of the stress felt by some students within the school environment. When interviewed, he described the La Salle school climate as a "veritable pressure cooker for some students." As a result, Mr. Talbot made a conscious decision to provide classroom experiences in which the study of psychology as a discipline would be combined with a personal or experiential approach. This personal component of his course is offered with restraint and caution in that classes engage in such experiences only upon student request, and, in any given activity, Mr. Talbot attempts to make certain that students are comfortable in "opting out." In practice, this has meant that while the vast majority of courses that constitute the curriculum confine their work to the formal and academic, students in a few classes can deal with one another at personal and interpersonal levels.

Mr. Talbot perceives that the provision of opportunities for a relatively few students to escape from the rigorous academic schedule is a functional necessity for some students. In fact, he expressed the view that contemporary high schools need what he describes as an "underground counseling system." All high school faculties surely include certain adults who are especially gifted at communicating and maintaining extended role relationships with students. At La Salle, this "underground system" is not extensive but includes certain teachers and administrators with whom a student can readily identify because of their willingness to extend their professional roles beyond the explicit academic mission of the school.

DEFINING ACADEMIC STANDARDS

As already indicated, La Salle High School courses function at four academic levels: Honors, A, B, and C. The La Salle rationale for segregating students on the basis of performance is the traditional position expressed by one of La Salle's administrators: "We want every kid, at their level, to experience success." Leveling or tracking, however, may be fraught with serious problems that can result from the psychological effect of labeling students—a "self-fulfilling prophecy" effect such as expecting too little of lower-track students and then getting little as a consequence—and the premature sorting of students, which may direct certain students to college while further educational options are severely restricted for others through their assignment to remedial or vocational tracks. In fact, the practice of tracking in high schools has been the subject of much serious and telling criticism over a period of years.[2] On the other hand, the option of not leveling students is often criticized on the ground that the curriculum must then be aimed at the middle of the student population and that the effect of this policy is to neglect the needs of the brighter and more advanced students and to provide curricular experiences that are too rigorous for certain students.

La Salle High School has chosen to implement what it calls the leveling system, but in a manner calculated to avoid at least certain of the potential problems conventionally associated with high school tracking. First, students are placed in different levels, but, as already indicated, their placement is to a large extent based on their performance, a variable over which students do have a measure of control. Second, the process of placing students is accomplished on a department by department basis, and the net result is that a large majority of students have classes on at least two levels and therefore cannot be categorized easily, for example, as B level or C level. (Only about 50 of the school's 2,000 students have all their classes at the C level.) Third, student performance is evaluated at the end of each semester for the purpose of ensuring student mobility. Fourth, a student's parents may override the school's recommendation for their son or daughter, simply by requesting a specific level. Finally, leveling does not reduce the student's future options significantly because each of the various levels, including the C level, is obligated to pursue the overall district mandate to achieve academic excellence. One study of La Salle graduates indicated that about one-third of C level students went on to college. Unlike students in the lowest track at other schools, La Salle students do not find themselves at a dead end academically.

Contrary to our initial expectations, in our comparison of the quality of instruction at the various academic levels at La Salle, we were impressed with its evenness, including the high quality of the instruction in C level classes. There, students were involved in academic work that was usually quite similar to the work being done by students in the other levels. History was still history, and science was still science. There were notable instances where the high-status department heads themselves undertook to teach C level sections. In fact, the primary differences between the levels appeared to be in the teachers' behaviors and in the amount of structure and guidance provided by educators rather than in the course content or the approach to subject matter. While in Honors and A level classes, the students took much of the initiative themselves, in the lower-level classes, the teachers provided more structure through the questions they asked and a more guided approach to assignments. In fact, however, a similar pedagogical approach and the same standards for evaluating teachers were used across the various track levels. It is clear that the mandate for academic excellence at La Salle extends to each of the levels and to the vast majority of students. Academic excellence is not perceived as a goal for certain academically able students in the school, with the less capable cast adrift; it is a mandate that seems to pervade the entire school and applies even to those students who are the least adept academically.

Oddly enough, virtually the only criticism of the system of leveling came from a few students who were consistently in the Honors or A tracks. Here and there, one could find the feeling that they were being identified as the "brains" and that their instruction was distinctly superior in an unfair way to those in lower levels. They appeared to feel uncomfortable in a role that they perceived singled them out for special treatment. As one of them said, "People who weren't in A track were set apart as not smart, and that kind of thing is not fair. Some of my friends were not in A track and they felt maybe downgraded because of it." Also, contrary to our own impressions, some students felt that instruction at the higher levels was in fact distinctly superior to that in lower levels. Should this be indicative of student sentiment, it may be a salient factor insofar as student morale is concerned, whether or not that impression is shared by outside observers.

THE LESSONS OF LA SALLE

While academic excellence is a widely expressed ideal of American secondary education, it is rarely pursued with such dedication or with such a high degree of success as is found at La Salle High School. The source of that success seems to lie in a number of factors:

1. The communities that La Salle High School serves not only express but appear to have genuinely embraced a commitment to academic excellence. With public accountability an ever-present reality at La Salle, that commitment cannot merely be nominal. At least as perceived by the professional staff, major deviations from that ideal will be exposed, and the consequences will be severe.
2. The chief executive officer of the school district is himself committed to that ideal and, to the extent that he has participated in hiring faculty and making key appointments, such as department heads, we find that ideal reinforced.
3. By and large, the commitment to academic excellence is not expressed in terms of mechanical learning of facts and skills. To a surprisingly large extent, teachers are able to reflect a high level of scholarship in their work. This, combined

with a student population much more attuned to scholarship or at least to higher academic aspirations than is commonly the case, makes it less likely that students will perceive the narrow academic focus as uninteresting or irrelevant. Whether or not these students' attitudes were built at home and simply reinforced through the ethos of scholarly commitment that pervades La Salle High School, it remains a salient factor in the school's success with respect to high academic achievement.

4. An extensive and closely monitored network of support systems keeps the great majority of students from falling far behind in their academic work and thereby becoming so alienated from and disabused of school that they drop out. While students are made aware of high academic expectations from the time they enter La Salle, they are also cognizant of the fact that they can rely on various mechanisms within the structure of the school should they require special help in meeting those expectations.

With some exceptions, the general atmosphere at La Salle High School is not so much one of genial camaraderie among students and staff as it is one dominated by a sense that an important professional service is being provided with a high degree of competence. This aura of professional competence is exuded not only by top administrators but by the superintendent's executive secretary, the teachers, the librarians, the counselors, and the teachers' aides. Education at La Salle is serious business.

In two perceptive critiques of American schooling, Ernest Boyer and John Goodlad used exactly the same titles for important sections of their books: "We Want It All."[3] Apart from the coincidence of the identical wording, both Boyer and Goodlad identified a crucial problem in American education. By expecting so much of our schools, Americans allow the schools' functions to become so diffuse as to detract from the quality of service to students. Implicit in their criticism is the obligation to choose the kinds of excellence we want our schools to embody. In short, we cannot have it all. For whatever reason, a clearly defined unity of purpose evolved at La Salle, and mechanisms were created to achieve a realization of that purpose. It is probably desirable that different schools, depending on a wide variety of circumstances, choose different kinds of excellence to pursue. La Salle High School is not an ideal school; but the kind of excellence that is exhibited there is worthy of consideration.

CHAPTER 9

Success and Failure in Educational Reform: Are There Historical "Lessons"?

The concluding essay in this volume takes a broad look at the way school reform proceeded over the course of the twentieth century and seeks to extract what might be called historical "lessons," from the record, although the term "lessons" must always be used cautiously. For one thing, educational reform comes in all sorts of shapes and sizes, and our experience with different kinds of reform may lead us to draw different conclusions depending on the nature and breadth of the reform being considered. Insofar as actual classroom reform is concerned, for example, our experience seems to indicate that those reforms that challenge the nearly universal desire for order have had very limited success. Order in one form or another, seems to be a staple of schooling as we know it, although, here and there, alternative schools have been reasonably successful in substituting a different kind of order for the traditional one based on teacher authority.[1] Reforms that conform to school structures, such as the National Science Foundation's emphasis on textbooks as carriers of a sharply modified curriculum, tend to find their way into school practice more readily than reforms that break with school norms. Another factor is the general social and political climate, which often militates against certain kinds of reform and enhances the fortunes of others.

Although the predominant tradition in educational research is scientific, history has a role to play in shaping educational policy, particularly by providing contextual clues as to what succeeds and what fails. It may be that one of the reasons for the failure of educational research to provide useful generalizations as to "what works" is that schooling is supremely contextual, and generalizations that are abstracted from the particular settings in which they are generated tend to lose their potency. History is no better than social science research in framing such generalizations, but rather than applying generalizations willy-nilly to schools everywhere, school reformers would be wise to formulate their stratagems with contextual clues in mind in much the same way that historians frame their interpretations.

Even early in the twentieth century when enthusiasm for reform was at its height and reputations were being made by proposals of all sorts to modify and in many instances revolutionize common practice in education, there already existed a pale cast of pessimism as to whether the proposed innovative practices would actually make their way into schools and, if they did, whether they would endure. Since then, the terms "fads and frills" and "pendulum swings" have become commonplace characterizations of the efforts to reform school practice. While present efforts to improve school practice continue unabated and at a time when we hear calls from every side about the mediocrity of American schooling, there remains not just a barely concealed pessimism but almost a cynicism about the chances for success in changing pedagogical practice. Two of the nagging questions, then, are whether this pessimism about educational reform is warranted and, if it is, why some common educational practices are so resistant to change. Beyond those questions is the related phenomenon of "pendulum swings" and whether and in what sense that rather cynical view of educational reform may or may not have any substance. And finally, there is the question of whether there are any lessons to be derived from previous efforts at reform.

THREE INSTANCES OF REFORM EFFORTS

Let me begin by alluding to three historically familiar examples of educational reforms: In the first instance, there are what might be called grand reforms of the sort we associate with that revered educational reformer, Horace Mann, to create a system of common schools at public expense as well as the expansion of that system into the domain of secondary education. Reforms like these attempt to restructure a whole national system of education.[2] There are also distinctive reform movements such as the effort in the early part of the twentieth century to make education more child-centered through a campaign that called into question certain fundamental assumptions about the educational process. In this second kind of reform, we are asked to reconfigure patterns of teaching and learning that have been practiced for as long as we have records of formal schooling. Finally, there is the specific change usually based on real or alleged research findings such as the urging on the part of various educational experts in relatively recent times that teachers organize their teaching by beginning with definite and explicitly stated educational objectives variously called behavioral objectives, performance objectives, and the like.

If we ask whether these reforms succeeded or failed, we are forced (as usual) to qualify our answer, but in different ways. Indisputably, we now have almost a universal system of common schools that is supported by public taxation. There is hardly a child in America today between, say, age 6 and 16 who is not enrolled in school. The question, however, is whether that reform succeeded because Horace Mann adduced persuasive arguments on behalf of the common school or because of his accession to a position of such power that he personally could implement that reform. When examined in those terms, it appears more likely that Mann's reform, if we can even call it his, succeeded because there were favorable social

conditions that made that reform seem plausible and set the stage for its implementation. To take one example of such conditions, Carl Kaestle has interpreted
the rise of the common school as the consequence of the ascendancy of middle-
class, capitalist Protestants who were able to maintain their privileges against a
fragmented array of political and religious minorities.[3] In this sense, the work of
Horace Mann as educational reformer leaves little room for optimism about de-
liberate educational reform, since his work can be regarded at best as a catalyst
for a change that probably would have occurred anyway.

Along the same lines, the further question is whether universal education was
successfully extended to the secondary level. It is true that the percentage of 14-
to 17-year-olds attending school grew from something under 7% in 1890 to a
majority of that age group in 4 short decades. However, if we judge from critical
examinations of what goes on in secondary schools, such as Theodore Sizer's
Horace's Compromise,[4] Arthur Powell, Eleanor Farrar, and David Cohen's
The Shopping Mall High School,[5] Philip Cusick's *The Egalitarian Ideal and the
American High School*,[6] and Linda McNeil's *Contradictions of Control*,[7] the issue
of whether universal secondary education has succeeded becomes less clear. Each
of these serious studies of what high schools are like points to the conclusion that
the extension of popular education to the secondary level has been, if not a complete failure, at most a mixed success. The extension of universal education to
adolescents may be regarded as an administrative success in that practically all
adolescents in the United States spend a considerable amount of time in an institution called the high school, but the reform is something less than a success in
pedagogical terms.

The child-centered movement to reform classroom practices also succeeded
in some sense, but only within a limited sphere. In 1894, the acknowledged leader
of the child-study movement, G. Stanley Hall, was able to announce to the annual
meeting of the National Education Association that "unto you is born this day a
new Department of Child-Study."[8] At least 20 states founded child-study associations, and their meetings by all accounts were very well attended. But the question of whether teachers actually adopted the practices that the leaders of this
movement advocated is more difficult to answer. In *How Teachers Taught*, Larry
Cuban estimates that perhaps as much as 25% of teachers, concentrated in elementary schools, tried out a few ideas associated with what became known as progressive education with the result that a kind of hybrid developed between traditional and newer practices, and a smaller percentage, estimated to be between 5
and 10% (also overwhelmingly elementary teachers), actively tried to implement
the reform in a substantial way.[9] Even in its heyday, then, something like two-
thirds of all classrooms in the United States were left untouched by the tenets of
the child-centered movement, and, in any case, the modest steps actually taken in
that direction left little by way of a lasting effect. It is true that, compared with
say 60 or 70 years ago, schools have acquired an air of informality, which is ex-

pressed mainly in the attire of both teachers and students as well as the easy banter that now characterizes their interactions. However, these outward appearances of informality should not be confused with any significant change in authority relationships in the classroom or even in the percentage of teacher talk as compared with pupil talk, a percentage that has remained remarkably stable at least since the turn of the twentieth century. Classes are taught pretty much the same way, with what commonly is called the recitation as the predominant mode.[10]

Now to the third reform. Have classroom practices changed to conform to the injunction on the part of such leaders in the educational world as James Popham and Robert Mager that the stating of precise objectives is the indispensable first step in undertaking to teach a class? This reform is somewhat different from either of the first two in that research findings usually are adduced to show that this approach to organizing teaching is scientifically valid and that superior results in terms of student achievement (sometimes called output) are forthcoming. (I might add parenthetically, however, that the research compass in this case, as in other cases of research-driven reforms, actually points both north and south simultaneously.) In this case, I know of no formal study of its implementation, so I must rely on my own observations as well as the experience of the many teachers who inhabit my courses year after year. There are, I know, certain elementary schools where a week's worth of lesson plans are required to be deposited in the principal's office on Monday morning, and these lesson plans almost invariably call for the stating of objectives right at the outset. My informants tell me almost without exception, however, that these lesson plans and the objectives that go with them are strictly pro forma and that once inside the safe confines of their individual classrooms, teachers carry on their activities in happy disregard of what has been safely embalmed in the file in the principal's office. In this case, therefore, we get a modest appearance of success insofar as the innovation is concerned, but the success is more apparent than real. I should acknowledge, however, that conformity with this practice may differ by state or region. In a state like Florida, I understand, the practice of teaching has been much more bureaucratically formalized so that there may be at least outward conformity to the practice. Recent emphasis on high-stakes testing may also serve the purpose of keeping teachers in line.

Unlike the other two examples of educational reform I have cited, this last reform, I believe, fails primarily because it misconstrues the relationship between social scientific research and educational practice. The problem lies mainly in its failure to take into account the supremely contextual nature of educational practice. Reform, we are told on every side, can be achieved by attending to research findings that tell us what the best practices are and provide us with the best rules for running schools as well as for how we should all behave as teachers. This is a position, by the way, that Dewey, that ardent champion of educational reform, rejected.[11] He argued that laws and facts simply do not yield rules of practice.

Instead, their value lies in what he called "intellectual instrumentalities."[12] These are to be regarded not as specific guidelines for how to act in given circumstances, but as intellectual tools by which we can fashion our own pathways. "If we retain the word 'rule' at all," Dewey argued, "we must say that scientific results furnish a rule for the conduct of *observations and inquiries*, not a rule for overt action."[13] Science, in other words, does not tell teachers what to do; it offers them the opportunity to re-examine their practices in the light of certain findings. Apart from the rather tenuous research findings that are used to justify the practice, then, the explicit stating of educational objectives failed as a reform because it was simplistically derived from these findings and because its proponents undertook to bludgeon teachers (figuratively speaking, of course) into accepting a practice regardless of teachers' own sense of how teaching goes forward in individual classrooms. It superimposed rules of action on the invaluable lore that teachers possess about how education actually goes forward and, therefore, was thwarted at the point where so-called scientific results collided with the craft of teaching.

With these examples in mind, we can turn back to the question of whether educational innovations succeed or fail, but we also can begin to look at the question of what sorts of innovations tend to succeed or fail and in what circumstances. My point is that if we look at educational reform in general, we cannot give a very precise answer to the question of whether reforms succeed or fail, but if we look at the type of reform and ask ourselves with some specificity how and in what respects and in what circumstances these reforms succeeded or failed, we may begin to get some insights into the popular conception that educational reform is a rather futile undertaking.

WHAT FAILS? WHY?

When looked at in this way, it appears, first, that successful reforms are not simply someone's good idea; they are sustained by or are at least consistent with broad social and political forces in which schools are situated. For some kinds of reform, as in the case of the drive for a universal system of common schools, this favorable climate made it possible to issue regulations or even change laws consistent with the reform. In effect, in order to be implemented, this type of reform requires something like an edict from a law-making body, a school board, a superintendent of schools, or simply a building principal, providing, of course, that favorable social conditions are present. Modern counterparts to this type of reform would include new state requirements for testing of teachers or new regulations governing high school graduation. In contrast to that kind of reform, there are those reforms that involve what teachers actually do once they are safely ensconced inside the confines of their isolated classrooms. Whether this kind of reform is prompted by a fundamental shift in assumptions about what education is all about, as in the case of child-centered education, or is proposed as a consequence of real or alleged research findings, as in the case of behavioral objectives, there seems to be an identifiable resistance to anything approaching major alterations when it comes to classroom practices in particular. Even the standard-raising kind of reform, while it often has the appearance of success in terms of implementation, tends to fail once it crosses the threshold of the classroom door.

A number of hypotheses regarding this persistent phenomenon have been offered. Some despairing reformers appear to have accepted the idea that teachers simply teach the way they have been taught and not the way they are supposed to. Others think teachers are just a recalcitrant, timid, lazy, or ungrateful lot. One frustrated reformer, for example, expounding on the reluctance of teachers to embrace instructional television with sufficient alacrity, attributed it to teachers' "failure to recognize the need for improvement, fear of experimentation, unwillingness to give time, and disillusion or frustration with past experiences,"[14] as well as to a tradition of conservatism. The problem with that answer to the question of why educational innovations fail is that it is no explanation at all. It gives us no indication as to why teachers allegedly have these attributes.

My own hypothesis about the phenomenon of teacher resistance to change in classroom practices begins with some insights John Dewey had into this matter just around the turn of the twentieth century. Essentially, Dewey argued that the reason why many educational reforms fail is that there is a conflict between the purposes and standards that are inherent in the innovative practice on one hand and what he called "external conditions" on the other. In other words, there is an unappreciated and, for that reason, fatal mismatch between what we are trying to accomplish with our reform and the actual structure of schooling. As Dewey put it:

> It is easy to fall into the habit of regarding the mechanics of school organization and administration as something comparatively external and indifferent to educational purposes and ideals. We think of the grouping of children in classes, the arrangement of grades, the machinery by which the course of study is made out and laid down, the method by which it is carried into effect, the system of selecting teachers and of assigning them to their work, of paying and promoting them, as, in a way, matters of mere practical convenience and expediency. We forget that it is precisely such things as these that really control the whole system, even on its distinctively educational side. No matter what is the accepted precept and theory, no matter what the legislation of the school board or the mandate of the school superintendent, the reality of education is found in the personal and face-to-face contact of teacher and child. The conditions that underlie and regulate this contact dominate the educational situation.[15]

If we are going to understand why educational reform fails specifically at the classroom level, then, we need to know what it is about the particular structure of schools and of classrooms that causes this disgorging of even the most noble efforts to reform pedagogical practice.

Since Dewey made that observation 100 years ago, there have been some indications as to where those disabling factors lie. At the heart of the conflict between what Dewey called "external factors" and enlightened pedagogical reform, it seems to me, is the antagonism between two seemingly compatible functions that teachers are asked to perform: the keeping order function and the teaching function. On the surface, it makes perfectly good sense to maintain that one cannot really get down to teaching unless there is a modicum of order; hardly anyone would dispute that. But in practice, the injunction to keep order has become so supreme that it simply swamps the teaching function.[16] The conditions of schooling are such that we can be counted as a good or at least an acceptable teacher if our classroom is orderly. This keeping order function, for example, is threatened by reforms such as those advocated by leaders of the child-centered movement. Extending great latitude to children to pursue a wide range of activities has the potential for chaos. The most persuasive single reason I can adduce for the persistence of the recitation as the predominant mode of teaching is that it is a reasonably effective way of keeping order. Budding teachers are even told in some methods classes that they should spread the questions around so that students are kept guessing as to who will get the next question from the teacher. The teacher as question asker and the student as responder is a way of ensuring teacher dominance in the classroom situation. If students asked the questions or if they addressed one another rather than the teacher or if they engaged independently in discovery practices, the risk of disorder would be introduced, and the structure of school organization will not tolerate that kind of risk. The prevalence of worksheets, for example, is simply a more extreme although still familiar example of the same phenomenon. Worksheets are damnable pedagogically, but they persist because they are reliable instruments of control.

The short answer, then, as to why certain reforms fail—especially those that require a change in the locus of control—is that such a change threatens the maintenance of order, and the climate of the classroom as well as the larger work environment of teachers is not conducive to that kind of risk taking. Educational reforms involving changes in teaching practice fail with such monotonous regularity because enlightened reform rhetoric and the generosity of spirit that impels people to attempt to change things for the better simply come into direct conflict with institutional realities. Good intentions and even competence notwithstanding, teachers are absolutely required to maintain a precarious order, and only the very courageous are willing to risk its loss.

THE "PENDULUM SWING" PHENOMENON

Related to the question of which kinds of reform succeed and which fail is another historical phenomenon to which many interested observers have alluded, the phenomenon of recurring cycles of reform. Like the belief that educational reforms are doomed to failure, concern about recurring cycles or pendulum swings may be justified in some sense but is overstated. I have never been a believer in the dictum, for example, that history repeats itself. In one of his lectures to future secondary-school teachers, Emile Durkheim argued that the value of the study of history must be found elsewhere[17]: "At most [history] could put us on guard against repeating old mistakes; but then again, since the realm of errors knows no bounds, error itself can appear in an infinite variety of forms; a knowledge of old mistakes made in the past will enable us neither to foresee nor to avert those which will be made in the future."[18] To be sure, certain familiar problems may recur from time to time, but they always occur in different settings and with different actors, so whatever it is we can learn from the past must be reinterpreted in the light of those differences.

The example of a pendulum swing that comes to mind occurred roughly between the end of World War II and the mid-1970s. At a White House conference held on June 1, 1945, Charles Prosser, a veteran of the old vocational education struggles and a hero in the victorious battle over the Smith–Hughes Act of 1917, was asked to summarize the recommendations of the conference. I do not suppose we will ever know whether he actually summarized the proceedings accurately; but he did report the participants as holding the view that 20% of the high school population was receiving an appropriate college-entrance education and that another 20% was being well served by vocational programs, but that the remaining 60% was not receiving the life adjustment education they really needed.

In any case, what was launched by this declaration was that dismal chapter in the history of educational reform, life adjustment education. Like other reform movements, life adjustment education was in large measure a slogan system rather than a concrete agenda for reform, but two life adjustment conferences were held under the auspices of the Commissioner of Education, and we have at least a general idea of what that movement was about. Essentially, it was a revival of the old social efficiency idea that the principal function of schooling should be the adjustment (preferably the happy adjustment) of individuals to the social world in which they found themselves. In fact, the percentages of the high school population that Prosser originally used were soon forgotten in the enthusiasm for the idea, and in short order life adjustment education was being proposed for everyone. As in the case of child-centered education, we can only estimate how much of life adjustment ideology actually found its way into the classrooms of the country. There are some indications that it did here and there,[19] but what evidence we have suggests that it was even less successful as a movement in that regard than was the earlier child-centered movement.

The pendulum began to swing back rather slowly. Contrary to popular belief, an adverse reaction to the anti-academic and even anti-intellectual formula-

anti —

tions of the leaders of the life adjustment movement was already under way before Sputnik was launched on October 5, 1957. Two books sharply critical of American education were published as early as 1949: *Crisis in Education* and *And Madly Teach*.[20] A vitriolic attack on the anti-intellectualism of the American education establishment was published by a professor of botany in *Scientific American* in 1951, an article that drew 248 favorable responses. And in 1953, the historian Arthur Bestor capped a number of effective attacks on life adjustment education with his book, *Educational Wastelands*.[21] Apart from these attacks, however, people like Max Beberman at the University of Illinois and Jerrold Zacharias at the Massachusetts Institute of Technology were already working on programs of reform that were practically antithetical to life adjustment education. When Sputnik was launched, it served mainly to put education in the media spotlight and to make it more of a national issue than it already was. In concrete terms, it undoubtedly was a vital factor in the passage of the National Defense Education Act, which was passed in less than a year after the launching. The publication of Jerome Bruner's report of the Wood's Hole Conference under the title *The Process of Education* gave the new movement focus and its own slogan of sorts, "structure of the disciplines."[22]

The new movement was almost the polar opposite from life adjustment education in terms of what it saw as the proper role for schools in American society (hence its characterization as a pendulum swing), and it benefited from millions of dollars made available by Congress through the National Science Foundation (NSF) for curriculum reform. (Life adjustment education received mainly moral support from the federal government.) Along the lines of the Physical Sciences Study Committee, first formed in 1956, projects in chemistry, biology, social studies, and other subjects were initiated. With much media fanfare, the term "new math" came into vogue. Consistent with some of Bruner's recommendations, these new programs sought departures from traditional modes of teaching, especially rote teaching, and tried to substitute inquiry-based exploratory work. Perhaps mindful of past difficulties in getting teachers actually to change their familiar practices, administrators of these curriculum reform projects spent a large percentage of NSF funds on teacher training. By 1977, for example, approximately 45% of science teachers around the country had attended at least one workshop sponsored by NSF and over 30% of high school mathematics teachers were involved in such workshops.[23] One survey conducted in 1976–77 found that 60% of secondary schools and 30% of elementary schools were actually using science materials emanating from NSF projects.[24]

One reason, however, for this apparent success was the strategy on the part of several of the NSF-sponsored curriculum reform projects to concentrate on creating new textbooks. Other more flexible types of materials that were also part of the proposed reforms were not nearly as widely adopted. In effect, then, the structure of the disciplines movement did succeed moderately in changing portions of the content of courses, particularly at the high school level, but it did not shift the locus of instruction away from teachers and textbooks in the direction, say, of what was widely called discovery practices. In fact, one analysis of the effects of the movement concluded that "[t]eachers were influenced by external factors only to the extent that it suited them and their circumstances allowed it."[25] Once again, even in the case of a moderately successful reform (at least in its time), we find the degree of success limited by the seeming impenetrability of certain familiar teaching practices, such as recitation and the practice of teaching directly from the textbook.

How can we interpret this cycle of reform as distinct from the individual instances of reform I alluded to earlier? In my judgment, no single-factor explanation, such as the orbiting of Sputnik and the national reaction to it, seems plausible. Life adjustment held out the promise of a stable, smoothly running society by revivifying the long-standing doctrine that the secondary-school curriculum in particular was unduly academic, simply a holdover from elitist schooling of the nineteenth century, and needed to be replaced with a program of studies directly tied to the everyday duties of life. That professional educators, such as the National Association of Secondary-School Principals, were in the forefront of this movement was probably prompted by the fact that the New Deal administration in the 1930s had taken some initiatives, such as the Civilian Conservation Corps and the National Youth Administration, that threatened the preeminence of the public secondary school as *the* institution where youth belonged.[26]

The demise of life adjustment was the result not only of heroic efforts by people like Bestor or the public clamor that attended the launching of Sputnik but also, and perhaps primarily, of a distinct decline of the yearning for a return to normalcy after World War II, a change in the national mood that quickly gave way to the Cold War. The real or perceived threat of external aggression made normalcy an outmoded doctrine. While the major figures in the structure of the disciplines movement were, to my knowledge, not cold warriors, popular and political support for an academic curriculum rather than a life adjustment one came from the notion spread not only by the likes of Admiral Hyman Rickover but by the very language of the National Defense Education Act. Over time, how to do mathematics and physics became a more urgent national priority than how to bake a cherry pie (to use Bestor's favorite example of life adjustment ideals). A changed social and political climate, in other words, made the ideas of life adjustment education appear obsolete, even an anathema.

Unlike the life adjustment movement, much of the leadership of the structure of the disciplines movement came from outside the education establishment. Edward G. Begle, Bentley Glass, and Jerrold Zacharias, I assume, never had an education course in their lives. If nothing else, this new reform movement brought one highly significant aspect of educational reform into focus. While selected teachers were involved in some of the planning of the reforms, the large body of teachers who were supposed to bring about those reforms were, by and large, treated as consumers of external initiatives rather than actual partners in the change process. The change was essentially externally imposed. It should come as no surprise, then, that teachers used NSF-sponsored materials primarily to the extent that they felt it would fit their time-honored pattern of instruction and left off what may have been the most important thrust of the reforms. Two factors, then, were primarily responsible for setting limits to the success of the movement. First, large numbers of teachers simply did not share the visions of how to do physics or how to do mathematics that were emanating from the various sites of the reform projects. Second, as in the case of other reforms, willingness to undertake new practices extended only to the point where the risk of a loss of order began.

Finally, it should be said that neither the life adjustment movement nor the structure of the disciplines movement that succeeded it, was a return to something that had in any literal sense gone before. In gross terms, the change can be characterized as a switch from soft pedagogy to hard pedagogy, but although the doctrine of life adjustment education contained within it certain elements of earlier ideologies, especially social efficiency, its anti-academic and virulent anti-intellectual tenets had not been expressed in such bald and vehement terms in earlier periods. Likewise, the structure of the disciplines movement may in a very crude way have been foreshadowed by the work of the Committee of Ten,[27] and its leading spokesperson Charles W. Eliot, but in no sense were the reforms of the 1960s infused with a mental discipline orientation as were the reforms proposed by Eliot and his committee. To be sure, there was a distinct shift in pedagogical reform orientation in the later 1950s and early 1960s, but that change reflected social and political as well as pedagogical trends that were for all practical purposes unique to that period.

THE HISTORICAL "LESSON"

Let me conclude by returning to the question of what, if anything, may be learned from historical examples of the sort I cited earlier or from the lone example of what commonly is regarded as a pendulum swing. Historical lessons carry a quite different message from the implicit and even sometimes explicit lesson that a traditional social science orientation brings to educational practice. The message conveyed by the traditional research orientation, which I regard as misleading, is that the study of education can yield generalized rules of action.

That orientation undergirds many programs of teacher education. Prospective teachers enroll in programs leading to certification with the understandable expectation that, quite simply, they will be told how to teach. It is very difficult for the faculty teaching those courses to challenge such a widespread expectation, so they work valiantly in what often turns out to be a futile effort to fulfill it.

They try mightily to use educational research to convey the rules of good teaching that their students demand. What is much more difficult to convey is that teaching is supremely contextual and what is reasonable to expect from teacher education in those circumstances are not recipes for what to do in particular circumstances; rather it is the ability to use whatever "intellectual instrumentalities" we are able to acquire in the course of our education as teachers to make wise judgments and sophisticated choices in those unique contexts.

It is precisely this kind of "lesson" that the study of history can provide. In contrast to the widespread acceptance, even reverence, accorded to scientific research, history holds a rather peculiar place in the educational world. It is not exactly ignored; in fact, there is a kind of ritualistic obeisance paid to it. Many textbooks and yearbooks on various themes in education, for example, begin with an obligatory historical chapter on the subject. But if history does not repeat itself and we cannot use it as a reliable guide to avoiding mistakes, as Durkheim suggests, then what really can it offer by way of illumination on problems such as those I have alluded to here? In my view, if there is something that legitimately can be called a lesson, it derives not from the substance of the issues but from the way they are treated. Reforms that entail pedagogical practice require all those involved, researchers and practitioners alike, as Dewey implied, to reinterpret the data for themselves in the light of the particular circumstances in which the problem is embedded. This means that teachers are not simply the compliant beneficiaries of research findings passed on to them by others; they are compelled by the nature of their work as teachers to reinterpret those findings in the light of situationally determined characteristics. Just as we are all obligated to be historians by virtue of the vagaries of memory and by the universal human impulse to *teachers' role* create order out of raw experience, so are we all obligated to be interpreters of the way in which research findings in education resonate with our own unique mix of students, subject matter, setting, and teacher characteristics. The central lesson that educational reformers can derive from historical antecedents is that pedagogical practice is highly contextual, making the success of every reform contingent on the extent to which it can be interpreted and adapted in the light of particular conditions. In this respect, the lessons of history are not very different from lessons that are derived and properly interpreted from avowedly scientific investigations of the teaching process.

Notes

INTRODUCTION

1. W. W. Charters, "Regulating the Project," *Journal of Educational Research* 5 (March 1922): 245.

2. A perceptive analysis of the effects of standardized testing is presented by Linda M. McNeil, *Contradictions of School Reform: Educational Costs of Standardized Testing* (New York: Routledge, 2000).

3. Jacques Steinberg, "Student Failure Causes States to Retool Testing Programs," *New York Times* (December 22, 2000): 1.

4. David Angus and Jeffrey Mirel, *The Failed Promise of the American High School, 1890–1995* (New York: Teachers College Press, 1999).

5. Diane Ravitch, *Left Back: A Century of Failed School Reforms* (New York: Simon & Schuster, 2000).

6. David Tyack and Larry Cuban, *Tinkering Toward Utopia: A Century of Public School Reform* (Cambridge, Mass.: Harvard University Press, 1995).

7. Joseph Mayer Rice, *The Public School System of the United States* (New York: Century, 1893); Joseph Mayer Rice, *Scientific Management in Education* (New York: Hinds, Noble and Eldridge, 1912).

8. National Education Association, *Report of the Committee on Secondary School Studies* (Washington, D.C.: Government Printing Office, 1893).

9. William Torrey Harris, "What Shall the Public Schools Teach?" *The Forum* 4 (February 1888): 573–81.

10. William Heard Kilpatrick, "The Project Method," *Teachers College Record* 19 (September 1918): 319–35.

11. I explored this concept in some detail in Herbert M. Kliebard, *Schooled to Work: Vocationalism and the American Curriculum, 1876–1946* (New York: Teachers College Press, 1999).

CHAPTER 1

1. John Dewey, "The Situation as Regards the Course of Study," *Journal of the Proceedings and Addresses of the Fortieth Annual Meeting of the National Education Association* (1901): 337–38.

2. David Tyack and William Tobin refer to "the 'grammar' of schooling" in their article, "The 'Grammar' of Schooling: Why Has It Been So Hard to Change?" *American Educational Research Journal* 31 (Fall 1994): 453–79. Their concept of "grammar" is virtually identical to what I mean by "the structural features of schooling." Tyack and Tobin use part of the same quotation by Dewey in order to introduce the concept.

3. Colyer Meriwether, *Our Colonial Curriculum, 1607–1776* (Washington, D.C.: Capital Publishing Co., 1907).

4. J. L. Pickard, "Course of Instruction for Our Schools: Number One," *Wisconsin Journal of Education* 1 (March 1856): 13.

5. J. L. Pickard, "Course of Instruction for Our Schools: Number Two," *Wisconsin Journal of Education* 1 (April 1856): 49. This style of curriculum writing was dominant in the nineteenth century. William Torrey Harris, for example, who was superintendent of schools in St. Louis between 1868 and 1880 and U.S. Commissioner of Education from 1889 to 1906, once extolled the virtues of grammar as a school subject by declaring that it "lets in a flood of light for the explanation of all problems which human experience can enunciate." See William Torrey Harris, "What Shall the Public Schools Teach?" *The Forum* 4 (February 1888): 576.

6. Wayne E. Fuller, *The Old Country School: The Story of Rural Education in the Middle West* (Chicago: University of Chicago Press, 1982): 93.

7. Barbara Finkelstein, *Governing the Young: Teacher Behavior in Popular Primary Schools in Nineteenth-Century United States* (New York: Falmer Press, 1989): 42.

8. Mary D. Bradford, *Memoirs of Mary D. Bradford* (Evansville, Wis.: Antes Press, 1932): 100. Bradford was a country schoolteacher who later served as superintendent of schools in Kenosha, Wisconsin, between 1910 and 1921.

9. *Teachers' Daily Register*, Joint District No. 2, Scott and Marcellon, n.p. Columbia County Historical Society, Pardeeville, Wisconsin. The particular comment was made in 1880, but other comments are recorded beginning in 1870. Typical comments include, "Scholars quiet and orderly," "School very quiet," and "Orderly and industrious," but here and there a visitor would record, "School mom sweet" and "Girls very pretty."

10. *Proceedings of School District No. 3 of the Town of Otsego, Wisconsin*, September 2, 1867, n.p. Data relating to the Otsego school are derived from the earliest of eight school ledgers purchased by the author at an auction held at the farm home of Mrs. Hilda Benzine on July 14, 1991. An earlier essay derived from these data analyzes three major variables in the determination of teacher salaries during this period: gender, summer vs. winter term employment, and residency status of the teacher. See Herbert M. Kliebard, "The Feminization of Teaching on the American Frontier: Keeping School in Otsego, Wisconsin, 1867–1880," *Journal of Curriculum Studies* 27 (September–October 1995).

11. David L. Angus, Jeffrey E. Mirel, and Maris A. Vinovskis, "Historical Development of Age Stratification in Schooling," *Teachers College Record* 90 (Winter 1988): 213.

12. *Proceedings of School District No. 5 of the Town of Scott, Wisconsin*, Columbia County Historical Society, Pardeeville, Wisconsin.

13. See also Kliebard, "Feminization of Teaching."

14. Lewis S. Schimmell, "Reminiscences of a Former Hereford Schoolboy," *Pennsylvania–German* 8 (November 1907): 11–15. Reprinted in Finkelstein.

15. *Proceedings*, Otsego School District No. 3, n.p.

16. Born in 1826, Pickett was chairman of a standing committee of the State Teachers' Association on the Revision of School Laws. It was reported that "during twenty years of teaching (seven only in winter), Mr. Pickett has never once punished with a blow that caused pain, and has passed several entire terms with no punishment beyond a reprimand." See "Aaron Pickett," *Wisconsin Journal of Education*, 1 (New Series), 9 (Old Series) (August 1864): 46.

17. Aaron Pickett, "Gradation and Course of Instruction for Common Schools," *Wisconsin Journal of Education* 8 (December 1863): 183.

18. Aaron Pickett, "Gradation and Course of Instruction for Common Schools," *Wisconsin Journal of Education* 8 (January 1864): 213.

19. Aaron Pickett, "Gradation and Course of Instruction for Common Schools," *Wisconsin Journal of Education* 8 (June 1864): 382–83.

20. William C. Whitford, "The Grading System for the Country Schools," *Wisconsin Journal of Education* 10 (November 1880): 455–71; 10 (December 1880): 509–24.

21. *Ibid.*, 469.

22. *Proceedings*, Otsego School District No. 3, n.p.

23. Henry Clay Speer, "A Course of Study for Common Schools," *Programme and Proceedings of the State Teachers' Association of Kansas, and the Papers Read at the Session of the Association* (Topeka, 1878): 22–23.

24. J. W. Holcome, "A System of Grading for Country Schools," National Education Association, *Proceedings of the Department of Superintendence*, Bureau of Information Circular of Information No. 3 (1887): 138–40.

25. H. O. Johnson, "Discussion." National Education Association, *Proceedings of the Department of Superintendence*, Bureau of Information Circular of Information No. 3 (1887): 145–46.

26. Henry Clay Speer, "Discussion." National Education Association, *Proceedings of the Department of Superintendence*, Bureau of Information Circular of Information No. 3 (1887): 148.

27. William J. Shearer, *The Grading of Schools* (New York: H. P. Smith Publishing Co., 1898): 31.

28. There was also some experimentation with the school calendar. In 1881, for example, the minutes of the school board meeting indicate that a 3-month summer term, a 2-month fall term, and a 4-month winter term were agreed to. By the 1890s, a 9-month school year was more or less standard.

29. David Hamilton, *Towards a Theory of Schooling* (New York: Falmer Press, 1989): 42.

30. *Ibid.*, 21.

31. An intriguing analysis of this phenomenon is presented in Myra H. Strober and David Tyack, "Why Do Women Teach and Men Manage? A Report on Research on Schools," *Signs: Journal of Women in Culture and Society* 5 (Spring 1980): 494–503.

32. Fuller, *Old Country School*, 79–112.

33. Hamilton, *Towards a Theory*, 49.

CHAPTER 2

1. Du Bois's characterization was expressed in a commentary about an official mission to France by the President of Tuskegee University, Robert R. Moton, who was looking into the condition of Black troops still stationed there after World War I. Du Bois reported: "What did Dr. Moton do? He rushed around as fast as possible. He took with him and had at his elbow every moment that evil genius of the Negro race, Thomas Jesse Jones,

a white man. Dr. Moton took no time to investigate or inquire." See W. E. B. Du Bois, "Opinion," *The Crisis* 18 (May 1919): 9.

2. W. E. B. Du Bois, "Negro Education," *The Crisis* 15 (February 1918): 175. For a criticism of Jones's role in African-American affairs generally, see W. E. B. Du Bois, "Thomas Jesse Jones," *The Crisis* 22 (October 1921): 252–65.

3. Thomas Jesse Jones, "The Sociology of a New York City Block." Unpublished doctoral dissertation, Columbia University, 1904.

4. *Ibid.*, 114.

5. *Ibid.*, 72. Jones's Jewish subjects, of course, spoke not German but Yiddish. Although Yiddish is a Germanic language, it has its own distinctive alphabet, locutions, and literature. One can only imagine the Jews' reactions to the spectacle of a Welshman posing as a Jew by speaking broken German.

6. *Ibid.*, 11.

7. *Ibid.*, 28.

8. *Ibid.*, 40.

9. *Ibid.*, 51–52.

10. *Ibid.*, 55.

11. Franklin H. Giddings, *Inductive Sociology* (New York: Macmillan, 1901): 63.

12. Jones, "Sociology of a New York City Block," 91–93.

13. *Ibid.*, 133.

14. *Ibid.*, 131–33.

15. The historian Edward A. Krug was one of the first to draw attention to social service and social settlement work as a vital ingredient in what came to be known as progressive education. See, for example, his *The Shaping of the American High School*, Vol. 1 (New York: Harper & Row, 1964): 263–65 and *passim*.

16. Thomas Jesse Jones, *Social Studies in the Hampton Curriculum* (Hampton, Va.: Hampton Institute Press, 1908): 1.

17. *Ibid.*, 7–12.

18. *Ibid.*, 15.

19. *Ibid.*, 40–49.

20. Dorothy Ross, *The Origins of American Social Science* (Cambridge, England: Cambridge University Press, 1991): 122.

21. See, for example, Albert Shaw, "'Learning by Doing' at Hampton," *American Monthly Review of Reviews* 20 (April 1900): 417–32.

22. Social studies as a generic term to include history, government, political economy, etc., may itself have been Jones's invention. See Krug, *Shaping*, Vol. 1, 354.

23. Walter H. Eddy, "Final Report of the Committee on Revision of the High School Course," *Bulletin of the New York High School Teachers Association*, No. 5 (1910–11), 26–27.

24. Quoted in Walter H. Drost, "Clarence Kingsley—the New York Years," *History of Education Quarterly* 6 (Fall 1966): 18. The details of Kingsley's early career are drawn from Drost's article.

25. National Education Association, *Cardinal Principles of Secondary Education: A Report of the Commission on the Reorganization of Secondary Education* (Washington, D.C.: Government Printing Office, 1918).

26. Krug, *Shaping*, Vol. 1, 355.

27. Thomas Jesse Jones, "Statement of Chairman of the Committee on Social Studies," in Preliminary Statements by Chairmen of Committees of the National Education Association, *The Reorganization of Secondary Education* (Washington, D.C.: Government Printing Office, 1913): 17.

28. *Ibid.*, 27.

29. Committee on Social Studies of the National Commission on the Reorganization of Secondary Education of the National Education Association, *The Social Studies in Secondary Education* (Washington, D.C.: Government Printing Office, 1916): 9.

30. Frederick Winslow Taylor, *The Principles of Scientific Management* (New York: Harper, 1911).

31. Committee on Social Studies, *Social Studies in Secondary Education*, 13.

32. *Ibid.*, 17.

33. Krug, *Shaping*, Vol. 1, 400.

34. Murray Edelman, *Political Language: Words That Succeed and Policies That Fail* (New York: Academic Press, 1977): 58.

CHAPTER 3

1. National Education Association, *Cardinal Principles of Secondary Education: A Report of the Commission on the Reorganization of Secondary Education* (Washington, D.C.: Government Printing Office, 1918).

2. National Education Association, *Report of the Committee on Secondary School Studies* (Washington, D.C.: Government Printing Office, 1893).

3. Edward A. Krug, *The Shaping of the American High School*, Vol. 1 (New York: Harper & Row, 1964): 400.

4. G. Stanley Hall, *Adolescence*, Vol. 2 (New York: Appleton-Century-Crofts, 1904): 510–15.

5. National Education Association, *Cardinal Principles*, 7.

6. Lawrence A. Cremin, "The Problem of Curriculum Making: An Historical Perspective," in Arno A. Bellack, ed., *What Shall the High Schools Teach?* 1956 Yearbook of the Association for Supervision and Curriculum Development (Washington, D.C.: ASCD, 1956).

7. John Dewey, *The School and Society* (Chicago: University of Chicago Press, 1899): 19–44.

8. Edward A. Ross, *Social Control* (New York: Macmillan, 1901): 164–65.

9. Theodore C. Search, President's Annual Report, in *Third Annual Convention of the National Association of Manufacturers*, 1898.

10. John Dewey, "A Policy of Industrial Education," *New Republic* 1 (April 17, 1914): 11–12.

11. David Snedden, "Vocational Education," *New Republic* 3 (May 15, 1915): 40–42.

12. John Dewey, "Splitting Up the School System," *New Republic* 2 (April 17, 1915): 42.

13. National Education Association, *Cardinal Principles*, 22.

14. David Snedden, "The Practical Arts in Liberal Education," *Education Review* 43 (April 1912): 379.

15. National Education Association, *Cardinal Principles*, 9.

16. *Ibid.*, 6–7.

17. Jeffrey Mirel and David Angus, "High Standards for All? The Struggle for Equality in the High School Curriculum, 1890–1990," *American Educator* 18 (Summer 1994): 4–9, 40–42.

18. *Ibid.*, 7.

19. *Ibid.*, 41 (emphasis in original).

CHAPTER 4

1. National Education Association, *Report of the Committee on Secondary School Studies* (Washington, D.C.: Government Printing Office, 1893).

2. Wilford M. Aiken, *The Story of the Eight-Year Study* (New York: Harper & Brothers, 1931): 275.

3. *Ibid.*, 47

4. *Ibid.*, 512–16.

5. H. H. Ryan, "Experimental College Entrance Units: A Committee Report. I. Introductory Statement," *North Central Association Quarterly* 9 (January 1935): 345–50.

6. *Thirty Schools Tell Their Story* (New York: Harper & Brothers, 1943): 638–58.

7. Dean Chamberlain, Enid Chamberlain, Neal E. Drought, and William E. Scott, *Did They Succeed in College?* (New York: Harper & Brothers, 1942): xx.

8. *Ibid.*, xxi (emphasis in original).

9. Harl R. Douglass, "Education of All Youth for Life Adjustment," *Annals of the American Academy of Political and Social Science* 265 (1949): 114 (emphasis in original).

10. Vernon L. Nickell, "How Can We Develop an Effective Program of Education for Life Adjustment?" *Bulletin of the National Association of Secondary-School Principals* 33 (April 1949): 154.

11. "High School Overhaul," *Newsweek* 34 (December 15, 1947): 86.

12. Harry J. Fuller, "The Emperor's New Clothes, or Prius Dementat," *Scientific Monthly* 72 (January 1951): 34.

13. Arthur E. Bestor, Jr. "Anti-Intellectualism in the Schools" *New Republic* 128 (January 19, 1953): 12–13.

14. Charles W. Eliot, "The Fundamental Assumptions in the Report of the Committee of Ten," *Educational Review* 30 (November 1905): 325–43.

15. Boyd H. Bode, *Modern Educational Theories* (New York: Macmillan, 1927).

16. Arthur E. Bestor, Jr., *Educational Wastelands: The Retreat from Learning in Our Public Schools* (Urbana: University of Illinois Press, 1953): 51.

CHAPTER 5

1. George S. Counts, *Dare the Schools Build a New Social Order?* (New York: John Day, 1932).

2. David Tyack and Larry Cuban, *Tinkering Toward Utopia: A Century of Public School Reform* (Cambridge, Mass.: Harvard University Press, 1995): 85–109.

3. *Ibid.*, 186.

4. *Ibid.*, 182.

5. *Ibid.*, 183.

6. *Ibid.*, 188.

7. Harold O. Rugg, "Needed Changes in Committee Procedures for Reconstructing the Social Studies," *Elementary School Journal* 21 (May 1921): 692.

8. Harold O. Rugg, "How Shall We Reconstruct the Social Studies Curriculum?" *Historical Outlook* 12 (May 1921): 127, 184–89.

9. Report of the Committee of Seven, *The Study of History in Schools* (New York: Macmillan, 1900): 3–21.

10. Rugg, "How Shall We Reconstruct," 184–89.

11. William C. Bagley and Harold O. Rugg, *The Content of History as Taught in the Seventh and Eighth Grades: An Analysis of Typical School Textbooks*, Bulletin No. 16, University of Illinois, 1916: 58–59.

12. Neal Billings, *A Determination of Generalizations Basic to the Social Studies* (Baltimore: Warwick, 1929): 99–209.

13. *Ibid.*, 34; Harold O. Rugg and James E. Mendenhall, *Teachers Guide for "An Introduction to American Civilization"* (New York: Ginn and Co., 1929): 19.

14. Rugg, "How Shall We Reconstruct," 188.

15. Billings, *Determination of Generalizations*, 122, 155, 174–76.

16. *Ibid.*, 242–48.

17. All generalizations from *ibid.*, 34; Rugg and Mendenhall, *Teachers Guide*, 19. The source of the generalization is included along with its number.

18. Harold O. Rugg, *Changing Governments and Changing Cultures* (New York: Ginn and Co., 1932): 300–01.

19. See, e.g., sections on the American Civil War in Harold O. Rugg, *A History of American Civilization* (New York: Ginn and Co., 1930): 226–28 and on the Bismarckian Wars in Rugg, *Changing Governments*, 120–25.

20. Rugg, *Changing Governments*, 678.

21. Harold O. Rugg, *A History of American Government and Culture* (New York: Ginn and Co., 1931): 559 (emphasis in original).

22. Harold O. Rugg and James E. Mendenhall, *Pupil's Workbook to Accompany "Changing Civilizations in the Modern World"* (New York: Ginn and Co., 1930): 226–58.

23. Harold O. Rugg, *Changing Civilizations in the Modern World* (New York: Ginn and Co., 1930): 244–45.

24. Billings, *Determination of Generalizations*, 7–17.

25. See especially the social studies generalizations on poverty and accumulation of capital, *ibid.*, 141–45.

26. Rugg, *Changing Governments*, 188–90.

27. Bagley and Rugg, *Content of History*, 58.

28. cf. Fritz Fischer, *Germany's Aims in the First World War* (New York: Norton, 1967): 29–37.

29. Rugg, *Changing Civilizations*, 361–62.

30. Billings, *Determination of Generalizations*, 174; Rugg, *Changing Governments*, 34.

31. Rugg, *Changing Governments*, 1932 ed., 670, 1937 ed., 15.

32. Rugg and Mendenhall, *Pupil's Workbook*, xiii.

33. Rugg and Mendenhall, *Teachers Guide*, 2–13; Rugg and Mendenhall, *Pupil's Workbook*, xiii–xiv.

34. Harold O. Rugg, "Education and International Understanding," *Progressive Education* 8 (April 1931), 299.

35. Elmer A. Winters, "Harold Rugg and Education for Social Reconstruction." Ph.D. diss., University of Wisconsin–Madison, 1968.

CHAPTER 6

1. Arthur G. Powell, Eleanor Farrar, and David K. Cohen, *The Shopping Mall High School: Winners and Losers in the Educational Marketplace* (Boston: Houghton Mifflin, 1985): 11–12.

2. National Education Association, *Report of the Committee on Secondary School Studies* (Washington, D.C.: Government Printing Office, 1893).

3. Robert M. Hampel, *The Last Little Citadel: American High Schools Since 1940* (Boston: Houghton Mifflin, 1986): 147. The two studies are Ernest L. Boyer, *High School: A Report on Secondary Education in America* (New York: Harper & Row, 1983), and John I. Goodlad, *A Place Called School:Prospects for the Future* (New York: McGraw-Hill, 1984).

4. Roger Tlusty, "Curricular Transformation as Social History: Eau Claire High School, 1890–1915." Ph.D., diss., University of Wisconsin–Madison, 1986: 218.

5. Franklin Bobbitt, *Curriculum-Making in Los Angeles* (Chicago: The University of Chicago, 1922): 4.

6. *Ibid.*, 7.

7. *Ibid.*

8. John I. Goodlad, *A Place Called School: Prospects for the Future* (New York: McGraw-Hill, 1984): 48.

9. John Dewey, "The Situation as Regards the Course of Study," *Journal of Proceedings and Addresses of the Fortieth Annual Meeting of the National Education Association* (1901): 332.

10. *Ibid.*

11. *Ibid.*, 333.

12. *Ibid.*, 334.

13. *Ibid.*, 335.

14. *Ibid.*, 340.

15. *Ibid.*, 337.

16. *Ibid.*

17. *Ibid.*, 338.

18. *Ibid.*, 342.

19. *Ibid.*, 348.

20. Seymour B. Sarason, *The Culture of the School and the Problem of Change* (Boston: Allyn and Bacon, 1971): 35.

21. *Ibid.*, 36.

22. Katherine Camp Mayhew and Anna Camp Edwards, *The Dewey School: The University School of the University of Chicago 1896–1903* (New York: D. Appleton Century, 1936): 365–56.

23. *Ibid.*, 375.

24. *Ibid.*, 368.

25. Sarason, *Culture of the School*, 212.

26. *Ibid.*, 213.

27. Henry Steele Commager, "The School as Surrogate Conscience," *Saturday Review* 2 (January 11, 1975): 55.

28. Robert Nisbet, *History of the Idea of Progress* (New York: Basic Books, 1980): 4.

29. Commager, "School as Surrogate Conscience," 54.

30. David Tyack and Elizabeth Hansot, *Managers of Virtue: Public School Leadership in America, 1820–1980* (New York: Basic Books, 1982).

31. *Ibid.*, 106.

32. Raymond E. Callahan, *Education and the Cult of Efficiency: A Study of the Social Forces That Have Shaped the Administration of the Public Schools* (Chicago: University of Chicago Press, 1962).

33. Ellwood P. Cubberley, *Public School Administration* (Boston: Houghton Mifflin, 1916): 338.

34. Tyack and Hansot, *Managers of Virtue*, 135.

35. *Ibid.*, 142.

36. *Ibid.*, 153.

CHAPTER 7

1. I discuss this point in more detail in the preface to my book, *Schooled to Work: Vocationalism and the American Curriculum, 1876–1946* (New York: Teachers College Press, 1999): xiii–xiv.

2. *Punch*, November 9, 1895, p. 222.

3. E. D. Hirsch, Jr., *Cultural Literacy: What Every American Needs to Know* (New York: Houghton Mifflin, 1987).

4. *Ibid.*, xiii.

5. *Ibid.*, 146.

6. *Ibid.*, xiv.

7. Herbert M. Kliebard, *The Struggle for the American Curriculum, 1893–1958*, 2nd ed. (New York: Routledge, 1995).

8. Barry Franklin, *The Search for Community: The School Curriculum and the Search for Social Control* (London: Falmer Press, 1987).

9. *Ibid.*, xv.

10. *Ibid.*, xv.

11. John Dewey and Evelyn Dewey, *Schools of To-morrow* (New York: E. P. Dutton, 1915), n.p.

12. *Ibid.*, n.p.

13. *Ibid.*

14. *Ibid.*, 1.

15. *Ibid.*, 11.

16. *Ibid.*, 15–16 (emphasis added).

17. *Ibid.*, 287 (emphasis added).

18. John Dewey, "From Absolutism to Experimentalism," in G. P. Adams and W. P. Montague eds., *Contemporary American Philosophy: Personal Statements* (New York: Macmillan, 1930): 12–27.

19. *Ibid.*, 116.

20. *Ibid.*, 118.

21. John Dewey, *Democracy and Education* (New York: Houghton Mifflin, 1916): 138.

22. Hirsch, *Cultural Literacy*, 119.

23. *Ibid.*, 141.

24. Christopher Lasch, *The Culture of Narcissism: American Life in an Age of Diminishing Expectations* (New York: Warner Books, 1979).

25. *Ibid.*, 223.

26. *Ibid.*, 224.

27. *Ibid.*, 239.

28. *Ibid.*, 252.

29. Hirsch, *Cultural Literacy*, 82.

30. *Ibid.*, 103.

31. *Ibid.*, 104.

32. *Ibid.*, 93.

33. Arthur G. Powell, Eleanor Farrar, and David K. Cohen, *The Shopping Mall High School: Winners and Losers in the Educational Marketplace* (Boston: Houghton Mifflin, 1985).

34. Hirsch, *Cultural Literacy*, 20.

35. *Ibid.*, 21.

36. Powell, Farrar, and Cohen, *Shopping Mall*, 306.

37. Hirsch, *Cultural Literacy*, 21.

38. *Ibid.*, 25.

39. *Ibid.*, 26.

40. E. D. Hirsch, Jr., "Cultural Literacy: Let's Get Specific," *NEA Today* 6 (January 1988): 16–17.

41. Hirsch, *Cultural Literacy*, 26.

42. *Ibid.*, 131.

43. *Ibid.*, 59.

44. *Ibid.*, 133.

45. *Ibid.*, 128 (emphasis added).

46. *Ibid.*, 129.

47. *Ibid.*

48. *Ibid.*, 130.

49. Romiett Stevens, *The Question as a Measure of Efficiency in Instruction* (New York: Teachers College, Columbia University, 1912).

50. Arno A. Bellack, Herbert M. Kliebard, Frank L. Smith, Jr., and Ronald Hyman, *The Language of the Classroom* (New York: Teachers College Press, 1966).

51. James Hoetker and William P. Ahlbrand, "The Persistence of the Recitation," *American Educational Research Journal* 6 (March 1969): 162–63.

52. Susan S. Stodolsky, Teresa L. Ferguson, and Karen Wimpelberg, "The Recitation Persists, But What Does It Look Like?" *Journal of Curriculum Studies* 13 (April–June 1981): 123.

53. *Ibid.*, 126.

54. Kenneth A. Sirotkin, "What You See Is What You Get—Consistency, Persistency, and Mediocrity in Classrooms," *Harvard Educational Review* 53 (February 1983): 21.

55. *Ibid.*, 22.

56. *Ibid.*, 16.

57. Hirsch, *Cultural Literacy*, 142.

58. *Ibid.*, 141.

59. Linda McNeil, *Contradictions of Control: School Structure and School Knowledge* (Routledge & Kegan Paul, 1986): 167.

CHAPTER 8

The research reported here was supported by a grant from the Governor's Employment and Training Office of Wisconsin. The project was under the direction of Gary Wehlage.

1. Reba Neukom Page, *Lower-Track Classrooms: A Curricular and Cultural Perspective* (New York: Teachers College Press, 1991).

2. See, e.g., Aaron V. Cicourel and John I. Kitsuse, *The Educational Decision-Makers* (Indianapolis: Bobbs-Merrill Co., 1963); James A. Rosenbaum, *Making Inequality: The Hidden Curriculum of High School Tracking* (New York: John Wiley & Sons, 1976); Jeannie Oakes, *Keeping Track: How Schools Structure Inequality* (New Haven: Yale University Press, 1985).

3. John I. Goodlad, *A Place Called School: Prospects for the Future* (New York: McGraw-Hill, 1984): 33–60; Ernest L. Boyer, *High School: A Report on Secondary Education in America* (New York: Harper & Row, 1983): 43–57.

CHAPTER 9

An earlier version of this chapter was presented at the Holmes Group Conference, January 27–29, 1989 in Atlanta, Georgia.

1. See, e.g., Ann Swidler, *Organization Without Authority: Dilemmas of Social Control in Free Schools* (Cambridge, Mass.: Harvard University Press, 1979); Liba Hannah Engel, "The Pedagogy of Janusz Korczak in the Hadera Democratic School: Early Twen-

tieth-Century Reform in Modern Israel." Ph.D. diss., University of Wisconsin–Madison, 1999.

2. See, e.g., Carl F. Kaestle, *Pillars of the Republic: Common Schools and American Society, 1780–1860* (New York: Hill and Wang, 1983); William J. Reese, *The Origins of the American High School* (New Haven: Yale University Press, 1995).

3. Kaestle, *Pillars*.

4. Theodore R. Sizer, *Horace's Compromise: The Dilemma of the American High School* (Boston: Houghton Mifflin, 1984).

5. Arthur G. Powell, Eleanor Farrar, and David K. Cohen, *The Shopping Mall High School: Winners and Losers in the Educational Marketplace* (Boston: Houghton Mifflin, 1985).

6. Philip A. Cusick, *The Egalitarian Ideal and the American High School: Studies of Three Schools* (New York: Longman, 1983).

7. Linda McNeil, *Contradictions of Control: School Structure and School Knowledge* (New York: Routledge & Kegan Paul, 1986).

8. G. Stanley Hall, "Child Study," *Journal of Proceedings and Addresses of the National Education Association, Session of the Year 1894* (1895): 173.

9. Larry Cuban, *How Teachers Taught: Constancy and Change in American Classrooms, 1890–1980* (New York: Longman, 1984).

10. Arno A. Bellack, Herbert M. Kliebard, Frank L. Smith, Jr., and Ronald Hyman, *The Language of the Classroom* (New York: Teachers College Press, 1966).

11. John Dewey, *The Sources of a Science of Education* (New York: Horace Liveright, 1929).

12. *Ibid.*, 28.

13. *Ibid.*, 30 (emphasis in original).

14. Quoted in Cuban, *How Teachers Taught*, 51.

15. John Dewey, "The Situation as Regards the Course of Study," *Journal of the Proceedings and Addresses of the Fortieth Annual Meeting of the National Education Association* (1901): 337–38.

16. See, e.g., Cusick, *Egalitarian Ideal*.

17. Emile Durkheim, *The Evolution of Educational Thought: Lectures on the Formation and Development of Secondary Education in France*, trans. P. Collins (London: Routledge & Kegan Paul, 1977 [1904–05]).

18. *Ibid.*, 9.

19. Dorothy E. Bruner, "Life Adjustment Education: An Historical Study of a Program of the United States Office of Education, 1945–1954." Unpublished doctoral dissertation, Teachers College, Columbia University, 1977.

20. Bernard I. Bell, *Crisis in Education: A Challenge to American Complacency* (New York: Whittesey House, 1949); Mortimer B. Smith, *And Madly Teach: A Layman Looks at Public School Education* (Chicago: Henry Regnery, 1949).

21. Arthur E. Bestor, *Educational Wastelands: The Retreat from Learning in Our Public Schools* (Urbana: University of Illinois Press, 1953).

22. Jerome Bruner, *The Process of Education* (Cambridge, Mass.: Harvard University Press, 1958).

23. Richard F. Elmore and Milbrey W. McLaughlin, *Steady Work: Policy Practice, and the Reform of American Education*. Report prepared for the National Institute of Education (Santa Monica, Cal: RAND Corporation, 1988): 15–16.

24. *Ibid.*, 16.

25. Michael Atkin and Ernest House, "The Federal Role in Curriculum Development, 1950–80," *Educational Evaluation and Policy Analysis* 3 (October–November 1981): 13.

26. Herbert M. Kliebard, *Schooled to Work: Vocationalism and the American Curriculum, 1876–1946* (New York: Teachers College Press, 1999): 175–209.

27. National Education Association, *Report of the Committee on Secondary School Studies* (Washington, D.C.: Government Printing Office, 1893).

Index

About the Authors

Herbert M. Kliebard is a professor emeritus at the University of Wisconsin–Madison. Upon completion of his baccalaureate degree at the City College of New York in 1952, he began his teaching career at the Bronx Vocational High School. After serving in the United States Army Medical Corps between 1953 and 1955, he returned to teach at the Bronx Vocational High School for another year. Between 1956 and 1962, he taught at Nyack Junior–Senior High School in Nyack, New York. After one year as a research associate at Teachers College, Columbia University, he was granted a doctorate by that institution in 1963 and in that same year accepted a faculty position at the University of Wisconsin–Madison, where he has been affiliated with the departments of Curriculum and Instruction and Educational Policy Studies ever since. His teaching and research have centered around curriculum theory, secondary education, and, particularly, the history of curriculum. His awards include a distinguished faculty award from the University of Wisconsin, a distinguished alumnus award from Teachers College, the Outstanding Achievement Award of the John Dewey Society, and a lifetime achievement award from the Curriculum Studies division of the American Educational Research Association. His books include *The Struggle for the American Curriculum, 1893–1958*, *Forging the American Curriculum*, and, most recently, *Schooled to Work: Vocationalism and the American Curriculum, 1876–1946*.

Calvin R. Stone, the co-author of Chapter 8, is affiliated with the Madison, Wisconsin, public schools. Greg Wegner, the co-author of Chapter 5, is on the faculty of the University of Wisconsin–La Crosse.